Pascal Programming for Libraries

Recent Titles in
Contributions in Librarianship and Information Science
Series Editor: Paul Wasserman

Books and Libraries in Camp and Battle: The Civil War Experience
David Kaser

An Introduction to Online Searching
Tze-chung Li

University Science and Engineering Libraries
Second Edition
Ellis Mount

Environmental Information in Developing Nations: Politics and Policies
Anna da Soledade Vieira

Federal Aid to State Library Agencies: Federal Policy Implementation
David Shavit

Sex Segregation in Librarianship: Demographic and Career Patterns of Academic Library Administrators
Betty Jo Irvine

Missionaries of the Book: The American Library Profession and the Origins of United States Cultural Diplomacy
Gary E. Kraske

The Politics of an Emerging Profession: The American Library Association, 1876-1917
Wayne A. Wiegand

Foreign Students in American Library Education: Impact on Home Countries
Maxine K. Rochester

Academic Librarians and Cataloging Networks: Visibility, Quality Control, and Professional Status
Ruth Hafter

Activism in American Librarianship, 1962-1973
Mary Lee Bundy and Frederick J. Stielow, editors

Librarianship: A Third World Perspective
Rosario Gassol de Horowitz

PASCAL PROGRAMMING FOR LIBRARIES

Illustrative Examples for Information Specialists

CHARLES H. DAVIS,
GERALD W. LUNDEEN,
&
DEBORA SHAW

CONTRIBUTIONS IN LIBRARIANSHIP AND INFORMATION SCIENCE, NUMBER 60

Greenwood Press
NEW YORK • WESTPORT, CONNECTICUT • LONDON

Library of Congress Cataloging-in-Publication Data

Davis, Charles Hargis, 1938-
Pascal programming for libraries : illustrative examples for information specialists / Charles H. Davis, Gerald W. Lundeen, and Debora Shaw.
p. cm.—(Contributions in librarianship and information science, ISSN 0084-9243 ; no. 60)
Bibliography: p.
Includes index.
ISBN 0-313-25259-9 (lib. bdg. : alk. paper)
1. Libraries—Automation. 2. Pascal (Computer program language) 3. Turbo Pascal (Computer program) 4. Microcomputers—Library applications. 5. Microcomputers—Programming. 6. Library science—Data processing. I. Lundeen, Gerald W. II. Shaw, Debora. III. Title. IV. Series.
Z678.93.P35D38 1988
025.3'0285—dc19 87-32292

British Library Cataloguing in Publication Data is available.

Library of Congress Catalog Card Number: 87-32292
ISBN: 0-313-25259-9
ISSN: 0084-9243

First published in 1988

Greenwood Press, Inc.
88 Post Road West, Westport, Connecticut 06881

Printed in the United States of America

The paper used in this book complies with the Permanent Paper Standard issued by the National Information Standards Organization (Z39.48-1984).

10 9 8 7 6 5 4 3 2 1

Contents

Series Foreword

The introductory remarks that set the stage for a published contribution serve best when they swiftly encapsulate the rationale for the work and then move out of the way to allow the authors to get on with the substance. In reflecting on this volume's place in the scheme of things, I am compelled to restate the first two paragraphs of the foreword prepared for *Illustrative Computer Programming for Libraries,* an earlier work in this series published in 1981. They still explain the significance of what is proffered in this modest yet significant monograph.

In the evolution of a scholarly discipline, a normal assumption is that the prime intellectual supports are based in the theoretical and philosophical contributions. Here is to be found the body of thought which charts the way forward. Still, to follow the path there must be appropriate and detailed maps of the territory, for it is never enough to philosophize or to conceptualize. Truth is ultimately engendered only through implementation, and this calls for demonstration through example or illustrative models. Herein lies the rationale for the present volume.

There is already an abundant literature on the abstract utility and the theory of computers, and of computer applications to library and information problems. But there remains a paucity of clearly written exposition that translates the theoretical into pragmatic terms which make such application feasible. Librarianship stands in need of works which successfully bridge the technological promise of these resources and the unique requirements of library and information systems.

Since 1981 developments have come with unparalleled rapidity. Yet, what was then a pioneering work, continues in the present edition to be a salient contribution. In its revised form, it centers upon a new and powerful language which has come to be extremely popular and applicable for use with the ubiquitous microcomputers, for in its design it enhances structured programming and simplifies and makes more comprehensible the tasks associated with programming. Thus, this up-to-date revision continues to serve usefully as a practical introduction to using computers by library students and by librarians, through clearly explaining and illustrating the application of this important and generalized programming language to specific illustrative situations. Neither abstract nor theoretical, the book sets out to and succeeds in achieving its aim of aiding anyone to learn how to use programs in information work. In this way, the present volume remains unique and important as a manual and handbook for the uninitiated. Because it effectively assists libraries and librarians to exploit a valuable new technical tool, this book remains an unquestionably significant contribution to librarianship and information science.

Paul Wasserman
College Park, Maryland

Acknowledgments

We wish to acknowledge, with thanks, the advice and encouragement of our students and colleagues. Special thanks go to Gerald M. Carlson, formerly a graduate student at the University of Illinois, who prepared the Pascal version of the document retrieval progam using weighted-term search logic.

Introduction

Computer programming is and will remain a valuable skill for the foreseeable future, not just for those in computer science, but for all who are involved in the many applications that are emerging in contemporary society. The automation of libraries and information centers and the general techniques involved in information storage and retrieval are good examples of such applications.

In recent years the proliferation of off-the-shelf software has led some to think that a knowledge of computer programming might be less important for those involved with automation. However, to think that all the good ideas have already been formulated is much like the sentiment, expressed a long time ago, that we should shut down the patent office because everything new and useful had already been invented. Moreover, off-the-shelf software, while a highly desirable commodity for which development should be encouraged, does not always work. In these cases it is often the user who must fix or "patch" the programs, and a knowledge of programming is quite valuable even if no truly original work is required.

Often as much art as science, computer programming requires imagination and intuition in addition to logic and a sense of order. Fortunately, a number of higher-level languages (those closer to the natural languages that humans use) now encourage the imaginative use of computers while providing a creative freedom that is often missing from prepackaged software. The best of these languages permit creativity within a structured format and enhance our ability to document our work for future reference. Among the most successful and widely used are those that have been developed for use on personal computers as well as on large mainframes and minicomputers. Pascal is such a language.

This introduction to Pascal programming, in addition to covering the basic elements of programming, attempts to survey the basic concepts of computer data processing and its capabilities and limitations in such library applications as acquisitions, circulation, bibliographic control, information storage and retrieval, and technical processing. Writing programs and running them on the computer is emphasized.

When you finish this book you should have:

an appreciation of appropriate uses for computers;

an understanding of some typical library applications of computers;

a knowledge of the main concepts and vocabulary of computers, data processing, and automation;

skill in techniques of problem solving;

an appreciation of "good" programming style;

the ability to write simple Pascal programs.

Because all this is easier to learn in some context, we will be concentrating on actual program writing, the details of which you will probably forget within a few weeks unless you continue to program.

The fear that many people have of computers is understandable, if unfounded. Learning computer programming is something like using a system of public transportation in a country where one does not speak the language. Trying to get around in such a situation can be a frustrating and unnerving experience. Yet, since local children do it with ease, it can't be all that difficult.

As with the transport system, the best way to learn to cope with the computer system is to use it. Start out with some short, safe excursions and gradually expand your area of competence. Before long you will be wondering why it all seemed so awesome.

Computers perform operations on information, according to instructions provided by the people who use them. The set of instructions for a series of operations to solve a problem or accomplish some task is called a program. The solution, or set of instructions, must be clearly specified in an algorithm (a precisely stated, fixed, step-by-step process that leads to the solution of the problem). A program is an algorithm coded in a programming language.

Each computer is designed to perform a set of elementary operations, called the "instruction set" for that computer. Its machine language instructions are coded as strings of ones and zeros. Machine-language programming is tedious and error prone, and the programs do not transfer from one make of computer to another.

Assembly languages aid the programmer by providing short mnemonic names for the basic operations, but writing programs in assembly languages is still difficult and error prone, and the results are still machine dependent.

Higher-level languages are designed to overcome the difficulties encountered in machine and assembly language (at the expense of some machine efficiency). Here the vocabulary is closer to that in which we usually think, and a typical instruction will translate into a long series of machine-language instructions, thus making the higher-level programs much more compact. Moreover, the programs will run on a variety of computers.

Pascal is a higher-level or procedure-oriented language. It was designed by Niklaus Wirth to encourage students and others to write clearly organized, or structured, programs. Wirth named the programming language after the French philosopher Blaise Pascal, which is why the name is not entirely in capital letters, as are many other programming languages. The official definition of the Pascal language is given in *Pascal User Manual and Report*, by Kathleen Jensen and Niklaus Wirth, first published in 1974. Since then attempts have been made to add features to the original version. A major limitation of Wirth's Pascal is its lack of direct access files. Another concern is its restricted capability in handling text—strings of letters, numbers, punctuation marks, and spaces.

Many uses of computers, including most library applications, involve text manipulation; inverting first and last names, or searching for titles containing a specified key word, for example, require the computer to separate, combine, and compare strings of letters.

This text uses version three of the TURBO Pascal programming language, which has sophisticated text string manipulation capabilities. TURBO Pascal was developed by Borland International, and is available for a variety of microcomputers.

TURBO Pascal provides for convenient interaction between the programmer and the computer. It maintains program and data files, supports file editing, translates (compiles) Pascal programs to machine language (the ones and zeros the computer understands), and provides error messages if the attempted compilation is unsuccessful.

Pascal Programming for Libraries

1. Basic Program Structure

A Pascal program has three parts: the program identification, the declaration section, and the executable statements. Pascal uses predefined words (called reserved words) to indicate the start of each part. You may wish to refer to the program INOUT as each of these parts is discussed.

PROGRAM IDENTIFICATION begins with the word PROGRAM, followed by the name of the program. Many programs include, in parentheses, the sources for data input and for display of messages created by the program's execution. (INPUT, OUTPUT) indicates that data will come from the microcomputer keyboard and files; output displays will be sent to the microcomputer display screen.

The DECLARATION SECTION describes all identifiers which will be used in the program. Pascal programs may contain one or more of these six kinds of identifiers: label, constant, type, variable, procedure, and function. The identifier definition begins with the Pascal reserved word for the identifier: LABEL, CONST, TYPE, VAR, PROCEDURE, or FUNCTION. This section identifies objects which will be used in the computer program; proper identification makes it possible to retrieve and refer to these objects from various points in the program.

The EXECUTABLE STATEMENTS are what actually accomplish the work in the Pascal program. This section starts with the word BEGIN. There follow zero or more statements, each separated by a semicolon (;). The end of the executable statements, and of the program, is indicated by the word "end," followed by a period: END.

Putting all this together, the Pascal program structure is:

```
PROGRAM IDENTIFICATION;
DECLARATION SECTION;
```

```
BEGIN
     statements;
END.
```

ELEMENTS OF PASCAL

Pascal recognizes twenty-six letters (a to z), and does not distinguish between upper case (capital) and lower case letters. The character set also includes the digits (0 to 9) and several special symbols: + − * / = < >( ) [ ] { } . , : ; ' # $ _ (underscore), and blank.

RESERVED WORDS

Pascal has thirty-five RESERVED WORDS which have special, pre-defined uses, and should not be used for identifier names. TURBO Pascal adds another eight reserved words, which are handled in the same way. TURBO Pascal reserved words are starred in the following list of reserved words.

```
*absolute    *external    nil          *shr
 and          file        not          *string
 array        for         of            then
 begin       *forward     or            to
 case         function    packed        type
 const        goto        procedure     until
 div          if          program       var
 do           in          record        while
 downto      *inline      repeat        with
 else         label       set          *xor
 end          mod        *shl
```

PROGRAM FORMAT

Pascal does not have rules on when to begin a new line, in which column a line should start, or which letters should be capitalized. However, programs are easier to understand and to correct if you use blank spaces to indent statements, forming groups or blocks within the program. Blank lines, which are ignored by the computer, also help human readers see the program structure. For example, program INOUT could be written as a single long line of Pascal code. Beginning each new statement on a new line and indenting statements which are subordinate to others helps the human reader see the logical flow of instructions that make up the program.

COMMENTS

Another human aid ignored by the computer is a comment. In Pascal, comments are either enclosed in curly braces—{comment}—or in parenthesis-star, star-parenthesis pairs— (*comment *). When the program is compiled, the { or (* is a signal to the computer to ignore everything until it reaches the next } or *); then to resume compilation. The comments between these symbols can, for example, identify the programmer and program date (always a good idea) or explain what is being accomplished (or intended to be accomplished) by the Pascal code at this point in the program.

2. Using TURBO Pascal

This chapter provides a step-by-step introduction to creating and editing files in TURBO Pascal. It assumes that you will be using a microcomputer with two floppy disk drives, one for the TURBO system disk, the other for your data disk. For complete descriptions of the TURBO Pascal options and editing commands, see Chapter 1, "Using the System," *TURBO Pascal Reference Manual.*

TURBO Pascal is available in versions for various microcomputers. Installation specifics vary slightly for different versions. This text describes procedures for TURBO Pascal 3.0 run on an IBM or IBM-compatible PC. These microcomputers use the PC-DOS operating system to support TURBO Pascal. Other microcomputers may use other operating systems—often MS-DOS. PC-DOS has commands which look like MS-DOS, but which generate different machine-level instructions for input/output. It is important to match your version of TURBO Pascal to the operating system of the microcomputer you will use.

GETTING STARTED

Insert the Pascal system disk in drive A of the microcomputer, and your data disk in drive B; then press the power switch to "on." If the computer is already on, insert the system disk, then press down the keys labeled CTRL, ALT, and DEL at the same time.

The red light on the disk drive will come on and you will be asked to enter the date, then the time. While these are not required to run TURBO Pascal, it is a good idea to enter at least the date, so that you will later be able to distinguish different editions of your work. After you enter the date and time [or simply press the enter key (↵)] you will receive the DOS (disk operating system) message and see the letter "A" followed by an angle bracket. This is the DOS prompt. (On a hard disk microcomputer you will see the letter "C" followed by an angle bracket.) You respond by typing "turbo." (Remember: capitalization does not affect any of these steps.)

```
A>  turbo
```

You will receive the TURBO Pascal copyright message and will be asked if error messages should be included. While the error messages take up computer memory space (1.5 kilobytes), it is a good idea to include them when you are writing new programs or revising old ones.

```
Include error messages (Y/N)?  y
```

You will see a brief announcement, "Loading TURBO.MSG," then the TURBO main menu:

```
Logged drive:  C
Active directory:   \TURBO3
Work file:
Main file:

Edit    Compile    Run        Save
Dir     Quit       compiler   Options

Text:         0 bytes
Free:   63485 bytes
>
```

LOGGED DRIVE

The angle bracket (>) is the TURBO prompt. Because we will be using the data disk in drive B for Pascal programs and data files, it is recommended that you change the logged drive to B. In response to the > prompt, type "L." When the system requests "New drive:" type "B" and press enter. If you do not change the logged drive you will need to specify the data drive each time you request a file. (Rather than INOUT.PAS, you would type B:INOUT.PAS.)

WORK FILES

The next step is to create a new file, which will be used for the program. Type a "w" in response to the TURBO prompt (>). TURBO responds:

work file name:

You type a file name (from one to eight characters). The file may have an extension—a period, followed by three more letters. The extension can specify the type of file. Initially, the two types of files we will use are .PAS, for Pascal programs, and .TXT, for text files which contain data for the programs. If you enter a file name without an extension, TURBO assumes the file is type PAS.

Once you have entered the name of the file to be your work file, the file is read from the floppy disk into the computer memory. If there is no such file on the disk, you will be told "New file." If you have a previous work file, which has been edited and the new version has not been saved (copied to the disk), TURBO responds:

Workfile B: FILENAME.TYP not saved. Save (Y/N)?

If you answer Y, the old work file is copied to disk. Otherwise your new work file replaces the old one, and editing changes on the old file are lost.

EDIT

TURBO's editing system is called by typing "E" in response to the TURBO prompt. You must have named a work file before you begin editing—you will edit the file which is your work file. TURBO's edit commands are based on those for *WordStar* from MicroPro. This discussion covers the basic editing and cursor control commands. Descriptions of all commands are given in the *TURBO Pascal Reference Manual.* (Editing commands can be changed from the WordStar default in the TURBO install program.)

When you are in the edit mode, a STATUS LINE appears at the top of the screen:

Line n Col n Insert Indent B: FILENAME.TYP

Line indicates on which line of the file the cursor is located. *Col* shows in which column the cursor is located. Use the cursor control keys on the right pad (← ↑ ↓ →) to move the cursor. *Insert* indicates that typing will cause the characters to the right of the cursor to be pushed to the right to make room for the inserted characters. To change from INSERT to OVERWRITE, press the CTRL (control) and "v" keys. CRTL-V again changes back to INSERT mode. *Indent* means that the auto-indentation feature is on—a new line will be indented by the same number of spaces as the line above. To turn off the auto-indentation, use CTRL-Q, then CTRL-L. B: FILENAME.TYP indicates that the file being edited is from drive B, its name is FILENAME, and it is of type TYP.

The control key (CTRL) is part of several TURBO commands. Alone the control key does nothing, but when you hold it down and press another key, special commands are invoked. It may be helpful to think of the control key as similar to the shift key—it is used only in conjunction with other keys.

The most important editing command is the exit command, CTRL-K,CTRL-D. This returns you to the TURBO main menu, from which you can, for instance, run your program. Basic editing commands are given in the following list:

Insert a blank line (line above current cursor position)		CTRL-N
Delete line on which cursor is positioned		CTRL-Y
Move text up one page at a time		CTRL-R
Move text down one page at a time		CTRL-C
Scroll up one line at a time		CTRL-W
Scroll down one line at a time		CTRL-Z
Move to bottom of file	CTRL-Q	CTRL-C
Move to top of file	CTRL-Q	CTRL-R
Find a specific word	CTRL-Q	CTRL-F
Exit—stop editing	CTRL-K	CTRL-D

Abbreviated commands such as page up, page down, home, and END are available on many keyboards.

SAVE

From the TURBO main menu or prompt, the S command copies the current work file to the floppy disk. If there is an older version of the file, it will be renamed FILENAME.BAK. If there was a previous backup file (.BAK), it will be erased.

COMPILE

The C command calls the compiler, which translates the current work file (assuming it is type .PAS) to machine language. The compiler checks for errors—for example spelling or typing mistakes. If you included the error messages file when you began the TURBO session, an explanation of the error will be included. You can press the escape key, move to the work file, correct the mistake, and resume compilation.

RUN

The R command compiles the current work file (if it has not already been compiled) and then runs the Pascal program. At this point the Pascal program uses data files and keyboard input, as appropriate.

DIRECTORY

To see a list of files on the disk use the D command. You will receive the prompt "Dir mask:" Press ENTER (↵) if you want to see all files. If you want all .PAS files, enter *.PAS, or use *.TXT for all text files.

QUIT

The Q command is used to exit from TURBO, returning you to the DOS level (B>). If your current work file has not been saved, you will be reminded of this and given an opportunity to save it before the quit command is obeyed.

PRINTING

To print what appears on the screen, be sure the micro is connected to a printer, and that the printer is turned on. Press SHIFT and PRT/SC (print screen). Move to the next page if your file is more than 24 lines (one screen), then SHIFT PRT/SC again.

TURBO Pascal comes with a program to provide printed listings of files. To run this program, "LISTER.PAS," you need to establish it as your work file (it is on disk drive A) and run it, as demonstrated below:

```
> W
Work file name: A:LISTER
Loading A:LISTER.PAS
> R
Enter filename: filename.typ
```

3. Input and Output

We humans need a way to communicate with the computer, to enter data and read results of programs. Information which is read by the computer while under the program's control is termed INPUT; any messages or results generated by the computer are termed OUTPUT. These two processes are often referred to together as input/output, or I/O.

For our purposes input generally comes from either of two sources: from the microcomputer keyboard, typed by the program user as the program runs; or from a data file on a floppy disk. Output is generally displayed on the microcomputer screen, although it can also be stored as a disk file or sent to a printer.

IDENTIFIERS

Pascal allows programmers to name important parts of a program. These parts are labels, constants, types, variables, procedures, and functions. Each is named with an IDENTIFIER unique within the program. TURBO Pascal identifiers begin with a letter or underscore, followed by up to 126 letters, digits, or underscores. It is generally advisable to choose identifiers sufficiently descriptive to express their purposes, but not so long as to induce typing errors. Remember that TURBO does not distinguish between upper and lower case letters, and so you can mix cases to improve legibility. Some examples of valid identifiers are:

Filname	total_overdues
week	PayPerHour

VARIABLES

Data to be stored or manipulated by the computer are handled in VARIABLES. A variable may be thought of as a designated, or named, portion of computer memory in which a certain type of data is stored. Only one item can be in a variable (or storage space) at one time. Arrays and records, which are more complex kinds of variables, are discussed in Chapters 10 and 14.

Variables must be "declared," or identified to the computer so that the storage space can be reserved, before anything can be stored in the variable. This is accomplished by the variable declaration part of the program, beginning with the word VAR, followed by one or more statements of variables and their types. The format for each statement is:

```
variable_name: type;
```

The variable_name must be a valid identifier. It is possible to declare more than one variable of the same type in a single statement. Separate each variable name from the next by a comma, but retain the colon between the variable names and the type:

```
variable_1, variable_2, variable_3: type;
```

There are many kinds of variable types. For now we are concerned with CHAR, STRING, and TEXT.

CHAR represents space for one character—a letter, digit, punctuation mark, or blank.

STRING is a sequence of one or more characters. TURBO Pascal allows strings of up to 255 characters. When a variable of type STRING is declared, its maximum length must follow, in square brackets, with no intervening blanks.

TEXT is the TURBO term for a text file. A text file contains characters organized into lines, each ending with a special symbol for carriage return/line feed (CR/LF). We will use text files to store data to be handled by Pascal programs.

An example of a variable declaration using all three types of variables is:

```
VAR
letter : CHAR;
line, newline : STRING[80];
fil : TEXT;
```

READING DATA (INPUT)

The basic instruction to get an item and assign it to a variable is READ. If input is from the microcomputer keyboard, the format is:

READ (variable);

READ instructs the computer to read characters from the input file (in this case the microcomputer keyboard). The characters read are assigned to the variable given in parentheses after READ. If the variable is of type CHAR, one character will be read. If the variable is type STRING, characters will be read until either the variable is filled or the end of the line is reached. When the next READ statement is encountered, the computer will move to the next character on the line, read the appropriate number of characters into the designated variable, and so on.

The READLN ("read line") command performs the same functions as the READ command, except that the rest of the line (whatever comes after the variable read) is skipped. This means that the next READ or READLN command will seek data from the next line of the input file. READLN can be used to skip the remainder of a line, or to jump over one or more lines in an input file.

Should the data be read from an external file rather than from the keyboard, it is first necessary to ASSIGN the file name to the file variable of type TEXT, then to RESET the file. See the program INOUT for an example of this process. Once the file is properly introduced in the program, READ and READLN can obtain data from the file. Input from a file is indicated by the file variable name before the name of the variable to be read:

READ (fil, variable);
or
READLN (fil, variable);

WRITING DATA (OUTPUT)

The basic output instruction is WRITE, followed in parentheses by expression(s) for computed value(s) and/or name(s) of variable(s) to be displayed:

WRITE (variable);

It is also possible to WRITE specific text, rather than the contents of variables. For example, if you want a message to be displayed on the microcomputer screen, you may specify the text to be displayed by enclosing it in single quotation marks in the parentheses following the WRITE command:

```
WRITE ('Enter name of data file');
```

The characters within single quotes are called a "literal string," and are displayed exactly as specified. If you should need an apostrophe (single quote) in a literal string, use two successive single quotes:

```
WRITE ('Don''t forget the file type!');
```

It is possible to write more than one variable or literal string, or to mix variables and literal strings. Each item to be written is separated from the one preceding it by a comma. For instance,

```
WRITE ('Right now ', total_overdues, ' is the value of total overdues');
```

is an example of the form:

```
WRITE (literal string, variable, literal string);
```

Remember, single quotes around each literal string. Note, too, the blank at the end of the first literal and at the start of the second; this provides a space on either side of the value of the variable.

The WRITELN ("write line") instruction works the same way as WRITE does, except that after WRITELN is accomplished, the next WRITE or WRITELN begins on the next line. WRITELN can be used without variables or literal strings to produce a blank line:

```
WRITELN;
```

PRACTICE PROBLEM ONE: INOUT

The first practice problem demonstrates the basic elements of input and output; once we have mastered these steps we can move on to manipulating or processing data. The program we develop will read lines of data from a file and display each line on the screen. When there are no more lines in the file, the program will end. We start with the most basic Pascal program, one which does nothing but begin and end. (In this and all programs in this text, Pascal-defined terms are in UPPER CASE, while progam-specific terms are in lower case. Remember that capitalization is ignored by TURBO Pascal, so this convention regarding capitalization has no effect on the programs executed):

```
PROGRAM inout;
BEGIN
END.
```

Remember the semicolon after each statement, and the period at the end of the program.

Sometimes you may need to stop the program before its normal end. For example, you may remember an error in the code you have not corrected, or a run-time error can create what is termed a "closed loop" or "infinite loop" which prevents the program from ending. To allow you to stop the program, include a user interrupt compiler directive just after the program name. The compiler directive is:

```
{$U+}
```

When the compiler directive is in effect program execution is slower, but you can stop the program by typing CTRL-C at any time.

The next step is to write something as part of this program. The easiest thing to write is a literal string:

```
PROGRAM inout;
{$U+}
BEGIN
  WRITELN ('This is a test.');
END.
```

Notice the use of indentation—the WRITELN command is bracketed by BEGIN and END.

Let's move next to reading the line from the keyboard; then displaying the same line. For this we need a variable in which to store the line after it is entered. We'll call the variable "line"; it will be a STRING of up to eighty characters. In this program we can refer to "line"—the actual words to be entered and displayed will depend on the operator who runs the program:

```
PROGRAM inout;
{$U+}
VAR line : STRING[80];
BEGIN
  READLN (line);
  WRITELN (line);
END.
```

It might be helpful to include a message alerting the operator that it is time to enter a line to be handled. Just after the BEGIN we might insert:

```
WRITELN ('Please type up to 80 characters, then press ENTER.');
```

Now we are ready to use an external file, rather than the keyboard, for the input. This step involves two more variables, the text file and its name. We have created two variables; "fil" is a text file and "filname" is a string variable which will be used to contain the name of the file to be used by the INOUT program. "Filname" can be up to twelve characters—a DOS file name of up to eight characters, plus a period, plus up to three characters for the file extension.

After the user enters the name of the file into the variable "filname" we ASSIGN that name to the file (the text file variable named "fil") and RESET the file.

```
PROGRAM inout;
{$U+}
VAR line: STRING[80];
  fil: TEXT;
  filname: STRING[12];
BEGIN
  WRITELN ('Enter name of file to be listed, e.g., inout.txt');
  READLN (filname);
  ASSIGN (fil, filname);
  RESET (fil);
  READLN (fil, line);
  WRITELN (line);
END.
```

Notice that the first READLN, to get the file name from the keyboard operator, does not specify a source for the variable; the keyboard is the implied source. The second READLN, however, includes in parentheses both the data file and the variable.

The final version of our program, however, must handle all the lines in the input file. If we knew in advance that there were nine lines, we could simply repeat READLN (fil, line); and WRITELN (line); nine times. This approach quickly becomes cumbersome, and in any case it is far from elegant. Pascal allows a more flexible approach, using a WHILE statement to control the execution of some other statement(s). We discuss such conditional execution in more detail later. For now, let us incorporate the WHILE NOT EOF statement. Here EOF stands for "end of file," and takes the form:

```
WHILE NOT EOF (fil) DO
BEGIN
  READLN (fil, line);
  WRITELN (line);
END;
```

In the first line we establish the condition under which the statement after it will be executed. This condition is that we are not at the end of the file call "fil." As long as this condition holds, the program will perform the next instruction, check to see if the condition is met, and if not, repeat the instruction, check the condition, and so on.

The next instruction in this case is actually two statements, enclosed in a BEGIN-END block. Because the READLN and WRITELN are grouped together, by the BEGIN (no punctuation) and END (semicolon) they are treated as a single Pascal statement, to be performed if the condition in the WHILE statement is true.

The final form of our program is now:

```
PROGRAM inout:
{This program reads and displays data one line at a time}
{$U+}
VAR line:STRING[80];
    fil: TEXT;
    filname: STRING[12];
BEGIN
   WRITELN ('Enter name of file to be listed, e.g., INOUT.TXT');
   READLN (filname);
   ASSIGN (fil, filname);
   RESET (fil);
   WHILE NOT EOF (fil) DO
   BEGIN
      READLN (fil, line);
      WRITELN (line);
   END:
END.
```

You will need a data file (file type .TXT or .DAT, for example) to go with your inout program. Use the TURBO edit program to create one. For your first effort, keep the file fairly short. You may want to adopt the practice of assigning your program file the same name you give the program in the heading (e.g., INOUT.PAS), and then assigning the corresponding data file the same name, with the .TXT extension (e.g., INOUT.TXT).

4. Formats for Input and Output

READING FORMATTED DATA

While it is useful to be able to read and display data, as program INOUT does, we need to develop a capacity to handle individual pieces of data—to distinguish authors' names from book titles, for example. Rather than handle the input file as a sequence of lines, we can look within a line for specific items. If the data file is organized consistently, with each like item occurring in the same place in an input line, the READ command can assign each item to its appropriate variable.

For example, consider a file of library books. This file will be called FORMOUT.TXT, in preparation for practice problem two. For each book the call number and author are recorded on one line, the title on the next. The Dewey decimal call number begins in column one, and can be up to fourteen characters long. There is at least one blank, followed by the author's name, in the format Last-name comma blank First-name blank Middle-name. We allow up to thirty characters for the name—any or all of these may be blank. Line two of each book's record has eighty characters for the title. Some of the books in FORMOUT.TXT are listed below. You may wish to add a few works to the collection:

```
020.54        Author, Ann
The Big Book of Best-Loved Library Stories
641.6         Pascal, Blaise
Blazing the Way; A Beginner's Cookbook
Fic           Nym, Sue Do
I Made It Up Myself
```

Because the file is structured, we can read each variable separately. The first step is to declare variables to hold each element of the book record. As we have carefully defined the length of each element, the following variable declarations will suffice:

```
VAR dui : STRING[14];
  author : STRING[30];
  title : STRING[80];
```

To read the elements into the appropriate variables, we need two READLN commands:

```
READLN (fil, dui, author);
READLN (fil, title);
```

Note that once the length of a string variable has been declared, the READLN instruction reads the appropriate number of characters from the current position in the input file. If the line ends (with a carriage return) before the declared number of characters has been read, the READLN stops at the carriage return.

FORMATTED DISPLAY OF STRING DATA

The WRITE and WRITELN commands can be used to display the FORMOUT.TXT variables in different orders. If we want author first, then call number, with the title on the next line:

```
WRITELN (author, ' ', dui);
WRITELN (title);
```

The ' ' between author and dui is a literal string of one blank. This is needed so that, if the author's name uses all thirty characters, there will be at least one blank before the call number.

How would you instruct the computer to display the call number and title (no author) on one line? The TURBO display wraps characters more than eighty onto a second line.

Unless instructed otherwise, WRITE displays a string variable with the first character in the current output position (the beginning of the line, or where the last variable or literal ended).

It is possible to right justify a string display by specifying the number of characters to be used with a colon after the variable in the WRITE command:

```
WRITE (author:30);
```

The last non-blank character in the string is placed in the position the number specifies, and blanks are used to the left of the string, to "pad" the format. Compare the results of the following WRITE commands:

	Column 1	Column 30
WRITE (author);	**Sirot, Elizabeth W.**	
WRITE (author:30);		**Sirot, Elizabeth W.**

PRACTICE PROBLEM TWO: FORMOUT

Write a program to read in and print book records. The records consist of three data fields, each of fixed length: a call number of fourteen characters, an author statement of thirty characters, and the title of eighty characters, on the next line. (See FORMOUT.TXT for an example.) Print each record so that the call number is in column one, the author in the same line, right justified (ending in column 45), and the title is starting on the next line, indented six spaces. Put a blank line between records.

We can enhance the VAR declaration and the READ and WRITE commands in INOUT to handle the more elaborate requirements for FORMOUT. The data file for this program should be typed carefully, so that the call number and title each begin in column one, and the author appears in column 16 of the first line for each record. Use the TURBO editor status line as you create the data file. "Col" indicates in which column the cursor is located as you type. The resulting program, FORMOUT.PAS, is:

```
PROGRAM formout;
{This program reads and displays call number, author,
and title data, demonstrating string formats}
{$U+}
VAR fil: TEXT;
   filname: STRING[12];
   dui: STRING[14];
   author: STRING[30];
   title: STRING[80];
BEGIN
WRITELN ('type name of file to use, e.g. formout.txt');
READLN (filname);
ASSIGN (fil, filname);
RESET (fil);
   WHILE NOT EOF (fil) DO
   BEGIN
      READLN (fil,dui, author);
      READLN (fil,title);
      WRITELN (dui, ' ', author:30);
      WRITELN ('      ', title);
   END;
END.
```

5. Conditional Execution

We have written programs which execute instructions sequentially—one after the other. There are times when it is helpful to be able to instruct the computer to perform certain steps only while a given condition is satisfied. We encountered one such situation with program INOUT, in which data were to be read and written only as long as we had not reached the end of the input file. This sequence of execution can be displayed in a flow chart as shown in Figure 1.

The shapes of the various boxes in the chart are significant, but the essential point for conditional execution is the diamond-shaped box which asks the question "end of file?" This is the only box that has two outgoing routes; which one is followed depends on the answer to the question.

THE WHILE STATEMENT

In INOUT and FORMOUT we used the Pascal statement

```
WHILE NOT EOF (fil) DO
BEGIN
   <process>
END;
```

The general form for conditional execution controlled by WHILE is:

```
WHILE <Boolean expression> DO <statement>
```

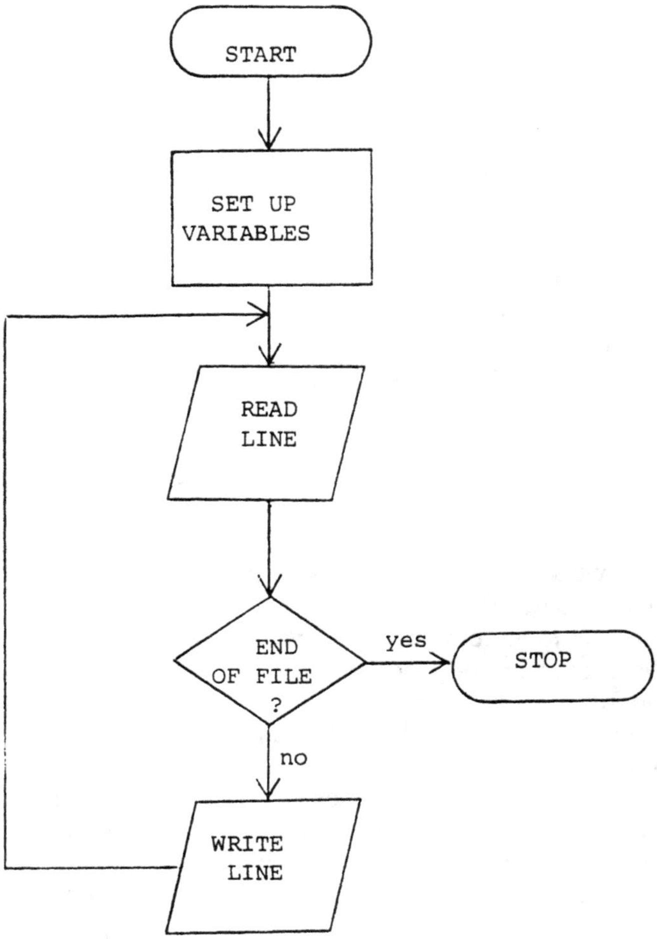

Figure 1
INOUT Flowchart

The <Boolean expression> must be an expression that can be checked to see if it is true or false. If it is true the <statement> following DO is performed, and the truth of the <Boolean expression> is again evaluated. This process continues until the <Boolean expression> is false, when execution proceeds to the step following the <statement> governed by WHILE.

Remember that a Pascal statement can be zero or more instructions enclosed in a BEGIN-END block. The READ and WRITE commands in INOUT were grouped this way, and performed while the not end of file (NOT EOF) condition was true. When the end of file was reached, the next instruction was performed—this was END., the conclusion of the program.

THE REPEAT STATEMENT

A similar way to control conditional execution is with the REPEAT statement. Here program flow is governed by the reserved words REPEAT and UNTIL:

REPEAT <statement(s)> UNTIL <Boolean expression>;

The difference from the WHILE statement is that the <statement(s)> is always performed at least once before the <Boolean expression> is checked. In addition, there may be more than one Pascal statement between the REPEAT and UNTIL. The <Boolean expression> is often a condition such as EOF (fil), meaning that the end of file "fil" is reached. As long as the <Boolean expression> is false the <statement(s)> will be repeated. The conditional execution of program INOUT could be written using REPEAT UNTIL, if we assume there will always be at least one line in the input file:

```
PROGRAM inouter;
{INOUT using REPEAT}
{$U+}
VAR line: STRING[80];
   fil: TEXT;
   filname: STRING[12];
BEGIN
   WRITELN ('Enter file to be listed');
   READLN (filname);
   ASSIGN (fil, filname);
   RESET (fil);
      REPEAT
         READLN (fil, line);
         WRITELN (line);
      UNTIL EOF (fil);
END.
```

Notice that we do not need to use BEGIN and END to bracket the READLN and WRITELN statements. This is because the REPEAT-UNTIL reserved words perform the bracketing function; all statements between REPEAT and UNTIL are performed as a block on each repetition.

THE FOR STATEMENT

Another Pascal statement that controls repeated execution of a statement under certain conditions is the FOR statement. In this case we must know how many times a statement is to be performed; we then use a counter to keep track of this performance, and proceed to the next instruction after the statement has been executed the appropriate number of times. The basic form of the FOR statement is:

```
FOR <control_variable>:= <starting_value> TO <ending_value>
DO <statement>;
```

The control_variable can be any ordinal variable (such as an integer or character variable), but it must be declared in the variable declaration portion of the program. When the FOR statement is first encountered, the value of the control_variable is set equal to the starting_value, then compared with the ending_value. If the control_variable is less than or equal to this value, the statement following DO is performed. The control_variable is replaced with its successor (e.g., an integer control variable is increased by one). The control_variable is again compared with the ending_value. If the control_variable is equal to or larger than the ending_value, the program moves to the next statement. However, if the control_variable is less than the ending_value, the DO statement is performed again, the control_variable is increased, and the comparison is made again. Consider the following example:

```
FOR counter:= 1 TO 5 DO
  WRITELN ('This is line number    ', counter);
WRITELN ('This is the sixth and final line');
```

The first WRITELN statement will be performed five times—the program execution will "loop" back to the FOR statement and check the value of the counter each time. When execution proceeds to writing "The sixth and final line," the value of the control_variable "counter" is officially undefined; that is, the programmer should not expect the value of 6 to be stored in "counter" after exiting the FOR loop.

THE IF-THEN STATEMENT

Another way to control program execution is to use the IF-THEN statement. As its name implies, a specified Pascal statement is performed only if a given condition is true. This statement has the basic form:

```
IF <Boolean expression> THEN <statement>;
```

Again, the Boolean expression is often a condition such as NOT EOF (fil), and the <statement> may be several Pascal statements bracketed by

BEGIN and END. If the <Boolean expression> is true, the <statement> after THEN is performed, and execution proceeds to the next statement. If the <Boolean expression> is not true, the statement after THEN is skipped. A simple example:

```
IF total_spent >2500 THEN WRITELN ('Overspent the budget.');
```

In this case, if the value of the variable "total_spent" is greater than 2500, the WRITELN statement is performed.

A more elaborate form of this statement is the IF-THEN-ELSE statement:

```
IF <Boolean expression> THEN <statement_1> ELSE <statement_2>;
```

Notice that there is no semicolon after statement_1. In this case, if <Boolean expression> is true, <statement_1> is performed and <statement_2> skipped; however, if <Boolean expression> is false, <statement_1> is skipped and <statement_2> is performed. For example:

```
IF total_spent > 2500 THEN WRITELN ('Overspent the budget!')
  ELSE WRITELN ('Only ', total_spent, ' spent');
```

THE CASE STATEMENT

The CASE statement selects one of several statements to be performed. It is especially useful when the user is to select an item from a menu, and the program's subsequent execution depends on the selection made. The general form of the CASE statement is:

```
CASE <expression> OF
  <value_1>: <statement_1>;
  <value_2>: <statement_2>;
  . . .
END;
```

When the CASE statement is encountered, the value of the <expression> is examined and the <statement> labeled with this value is executed. The <expression> is composed of an integer, byte, character, Boolean, or user-defined variable, or an expression composed of these types of variables, to yield an ordinal value. The <value> is a single value or list of values for which the corresponding <statement> should be executed. If the <value> is to represent more than one actual value, these may be listed, separated by commas, or the lower and upper bounds may be specified, separated by the Pascal subrange delimiter ". . ". TURBO Pascal allows the addition of an ELSE clause at the end of all cases; the ELSE <statement> is executed if the <expression> does not match the <values> listed.

Consider the following program, to help library users locate books. In this library the LC classification system is used, with the following shelving locations:

Basement—Call numbers B through N

Main floor—A and Z

Second floor—P

Third floor—Q through V

```
PROGRAM LClocate;
{use CASE statements to give shelving location}
{$U+}
VAR LCclass: CHAR;
BEGIN
   WRITELN ('Please type the first letter of the call number.');
   READLN (LCclass);
   CASE LCclass OF
      'A', 'Z': WRITELN ('Your book is on the main floor.');
       'B'..'N': WRITELN ('Your book is in the basement.');
       'P' : WRITELN ('Literature and fiction on second floor.');
       'Q'..'V': WRITELN ('Science, technology on third floor');
       ELSE WRITELN ('Please see a staff member for location.');
    END; {end case statement}
 END.
```

The CASE statement uses several features. The first case is a list of values separated by commas. The second and fourth cases involve lists of values with the lower and upper limits specified, using the subrange delimiter to indicate the intervening values. The third case is a single value, and finally the TURBO Pascal ELSE option is used to suggest assistance.

The diagrams in figure 2 provide graphic representations of the various conditional execution statements.

PRACTICE PROBLEM THREE: SIMPLE SEARCH

For the next problem we are to read in book records (Dewey Decimal call numbers, authors, titles, and publication dates) and then selectively display some of these records, according to the value of the first digit of the call number. In this case we want a listing of all books in science or technology—that is, those for which call numbers begin with a 5 or a 6.

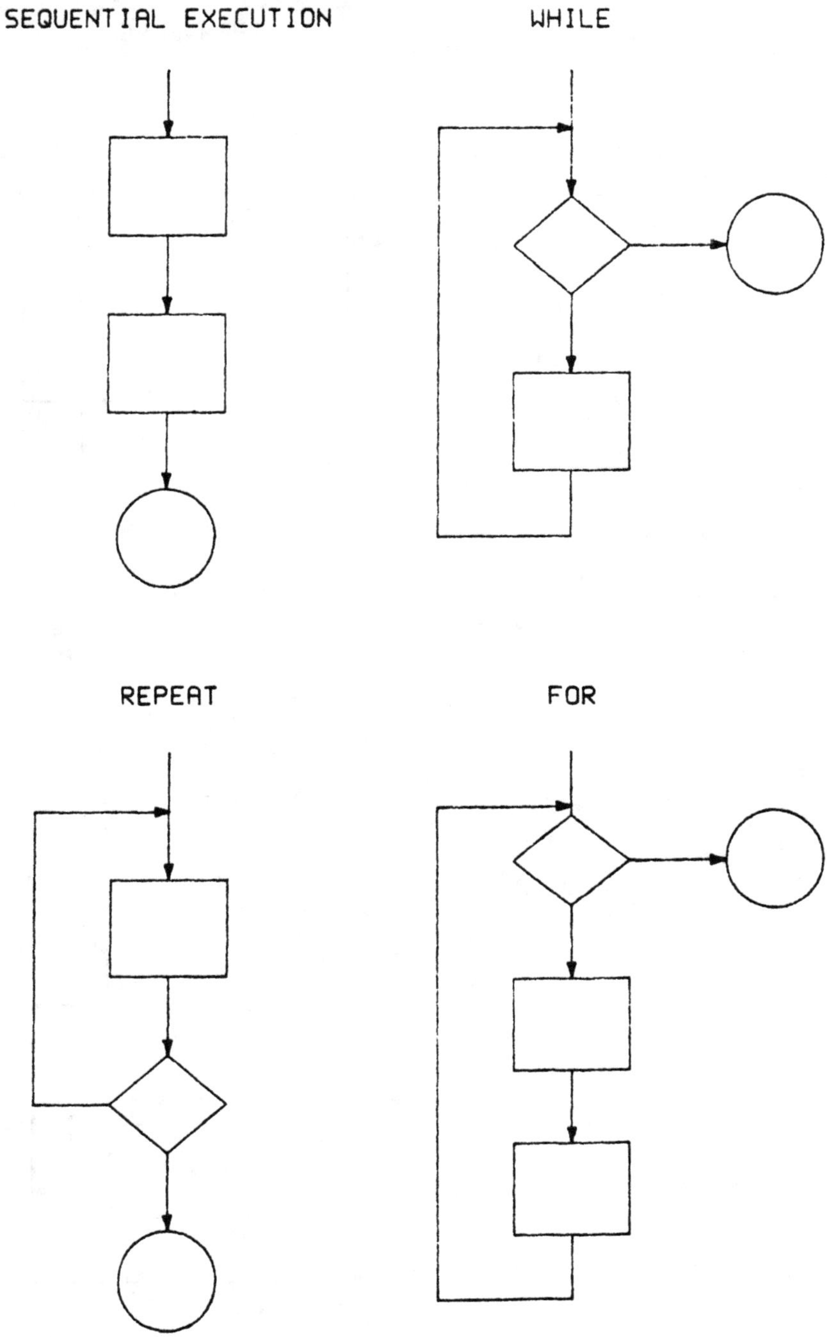

Figure 2
Conditional Execution Flowcharts

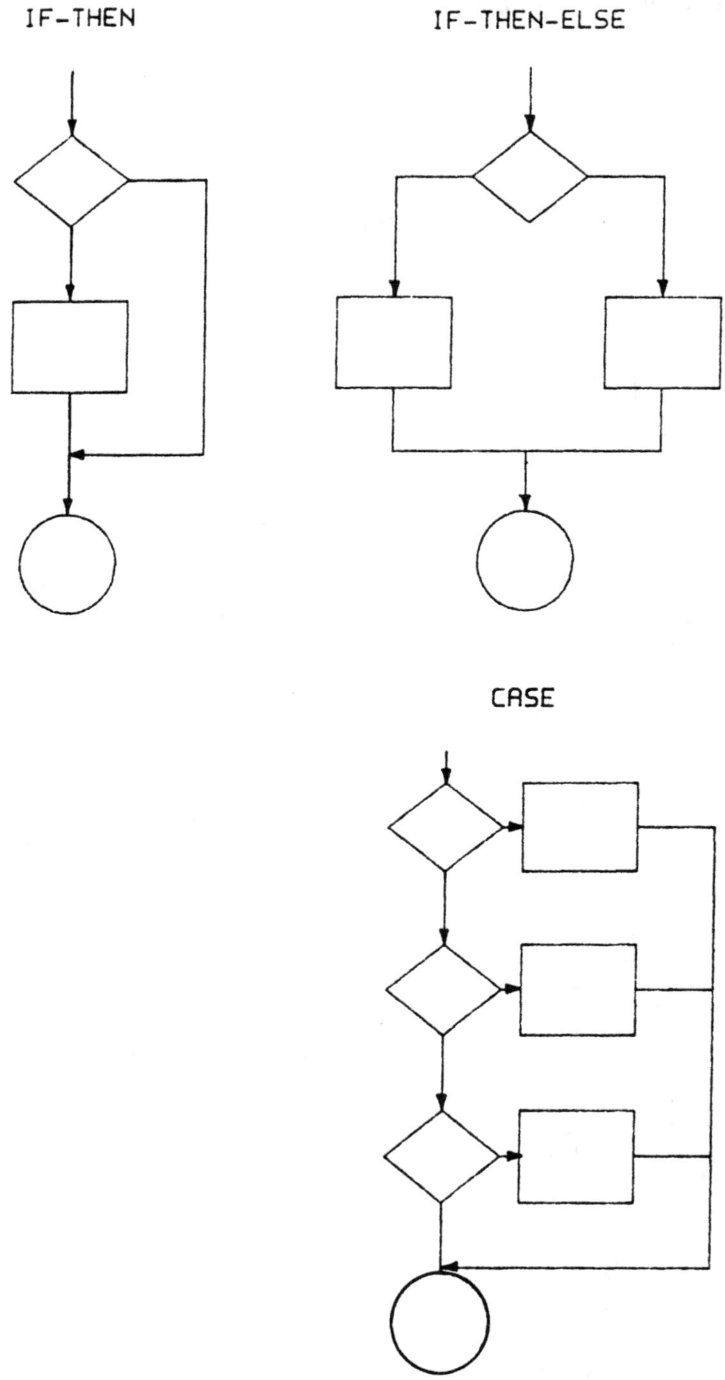

Figure 2—Continued

SIMPLE SEARCH ANALYSIS

The simple search problem is basically an elaboration of the INOUT problem. We need to impose a condition under which the output occurs—the presence of a 5 or 6 at the beginning of the call number. In order to test this condition, we will read that character of the record as a single character variable, to be checked. The data file for this program, SIMPLE.TXT, uses eighty columns per record:

```
034.65 DUI, MEL       HOW TO MANAGE YOUR LIBRARY GOOD                          1867
874.69 SMITH, FRED    DID YOU MANAGE TO FIND THE LIBRARY ?                     1964
543.89 SMITH, P.C.    COLLEGE CHEMISTRY MADE SIMPLE                            1984
078.2  SHERA, J.      ELEMENTS OF LIBRARY MANAGEMENT                           1964
384.2  JONES, W.T.    INTRODUCTION TO MANAGEMENT AND BUDGETS                   1982
043.1  ADAMS, R.      LIBRARY OPERATIONS, A SYSTEMS APPROACH                   1976
036.7  HO, ED         ADMINISTRATION OF LIBRARIES                              1979
674.9  BARNARD, C.    SURGERY FOR LEFT HANDERS                                 1972
623.2  DAVIS, C.      KNOW YOUR COMPUTER                                       1985
```

The SIMPLE.PAS program to read the book records and display those in science and technology is:

```
PROGRAM simplesearch;
{List books with call numbers beginning with 5 or 6}
{$U+}
VAR fil: TEXT;
   filname: STRING[12];
   dui: CHAR;
   rest: STRING[79];
BEGIN
WRITELN ('Enter name of file to search, e.g., simple.txt');
READLN (filname);
ASSIGN (fil, filname);
RESET (fil);
   WHILE NOT EOF (fil) DO
   BEGIN
      READLN (fil,dui, rest);
      IF (dui='5') OR (dui='6') THEN WRITELN (dui,rest);
   END;
END.
```

Note that the variable "dui" for the first character of the call number is declared as a character variable. Had we set it up as an integer variable, the instruction READ (dui) would have produced an error message, when a decimal value appeared in the data file. In order to handle only one character, we use a variable of type CHAR. Later in the program, when the condition is tested in the IF statement, the values 5 and 6 are placed in single quotes, as we seek to match the character '5' or the character '6' with the value stored in dui.

The output, as we run SIMPLESEARCH, is:

```
Enter name of file to search, e.g., simple.txt
simple.txt
543.89 SMITH, P.C.   COLLEGE CHEMISTRY MADE SIMPLE        1984
674.9  BARNARD, C.   SURGERY FOR LEFT HANDERS             1972
623.2  DAVIS, C.     KNOW YOUR COMPUTER                   1985
```

6. Numeric Variables, Arithmetic Calculation, Relational Operators

Computers were developed originally to compute: to perform arithmetic. Today computers are used for many other purposes, but the arithmetic functions, or "number crunching," are still important.

NUMERIC VARIABLES

Pascal handles three kinds of variables for numeric values:

Integer variables contain whole numbers. In TURBO Pascal integer variables must be between −32768 and 32767. Any computation with integer variables must have intermediate and final results within this range; for instance, 1000 multiplied by 100, then divided by 50, results in an overflow error because of the intermediate result, 100,000.

Byte variables are similar to integers, except that their values must be from 0 to 255. Byte variables occupy less computer memory than do integer variables—one byte as opposed to two.

Real variables include all decimal values—an integer followed by a decimal point and fractional value. Unless instructed to do otherwise, Pascal WRITES real variables in scientific notation, a real number multiplied by a power of 10. To indicate the exponent, Pascal uses the letter "E." When you see a real variable written in scientific notation, think of "E" as "times ten to the power of." For instance:

5.0E6 = 5,000,000

−6.0E−8 = −0.00000006

In TURBO Pascal real variables fall between 1E-38 (thirty-seven zeros after the decimal point, then the number 1) and 1E+38 (1 followed by thirty-eight zeros). The mantissa (value following the decimal point in scientific notation) can be up to eleven digits.

Real variables cannot be used to index an array (see Chapter 9), to specify a string length, or as the control variable in a FOR statement.

FORMATTED DISPLAY OF NUMERIC DATA

When TURBO Pascal writes an integer or byte variable, it automatically allows the number of spaces required for the value. For real numbers the default space allocation is eighteen spaces, using scientific notation. If INT = 7265, REALNUM = 5.725 and BITE = 4, then

WRITELN ('INT= ',INT, 'REALNUM= ', REALNUM,' BITE= ', BITE);

produces these results:

INT=7265 REALNUM = 5.7250000000E+00 BITE=4

It is possible to override these default displays by specifying the number of spaces to be used for each value. This is done with a colon, followed by the specified width (number of spaces) after the variable name in the write command.

WRITELN ('INT= ', INT:5);

will allow five spaces for the value of INT. If the value is less than five digits, blanks will be used to fill the spaces to the left:

INT= 7265

For real variables we can specify both the field width and the number of decimal places to be used. Decimal places are indicated by a colon and number following the field width specification. If REALNUM has the value 5.725, we can specify:

WRITELN (REALNUM:10, REALNUM:6:2);

which will produce the display:

5.7250E+00 5.72

scientific notation total 10 spaces used — 6 spaces (2 leading blanks), note that decimal places after 2 are dropped

For most library applications involving decimal values the results are easier to read if field width and decimal places are specified in the WRITE command.

ARITHMETIC CALCULATIONS

Pascal performs arithmetic computations, indicated by familiar symbols: + to add, − to subtract, * to multiply, and two kinds of division: / if a real variable is involved, DIV if only integer values are involved and integer division is desired. Thus:

707 + 6 = 713

62.5 − 2 = 60.5

11 * 6 = 66

131 / 4 = 32.75

131 DIV 4 = 32

Note that the result of integer division is a truncated integer value.

ASSIGNING VALUES TO VARIABLES

We have seen the Pascal assignment operator, := (colon, equal sign), in the FOR statement, discussed in Chapter 5. The ":=" should be read as "becomes equal to." Its function is to assign the value of what is on the right of the operator to the variable on the left of the operator.

```
counter := 1;
```

means set the value of the variable "counter" to 1. The assignment operator can be used to store the results of arithmetic calculations.

```
total := 5 + 17 + 6;
```

assigns the value resulting from the addition, 28, to the variable total. We can then use "total" in subsequent operations:

```
double := total * 2;
```

The assignment operator is used with all types of variables. However, the variable to which a value is assigned must have been declared to contain that type of value. In the examples above "counter," "total" and "double" have been declared as integer variables. An exception to this rule—that values must be the same type as the variables to which they are assigned—is that integer values may be assigned to real variables. (In a sense an integer is a real number without a decimal part.)

BOOLEAN VARIABLES

In addition to the numeric variables discussed above and character and string variables discussed in Chapter 3, Pascal uses Boolean variables. The value of a Boolean variable is either TRUE or FALSE. Boolean variables, like other types of variables, are declared in the variable declaration portion of a program:

```
VAR HasOverdues:BOOLEAN
```

Values may be assigned to Boolean variables using the assignment operator:

```
HasOverdues := TRUE;
```

If we have a data base of patron information, we may wish to take certain action for all borrowers who have overdue books. We can use an IF-THEN statement to determine which records to study:

```
IF HasOverdues THEN
  BEGIN
    [perform needed operations , e.g., send overdue notice]
  END;
```

RELATIONAL OPERATORS

Values of integer, real, byte, character, and Boolean variables may be compared with values of other variables of the same type, using relational operators. (Integer, byte, and real variables may also be compared with each other.) This comparison is called a Boolean expression, and the result of such a comparison is a Boolean value, TRUE or FALSE. The relational operators and examples of their use are:

=	equal to	2 = 2 (TRUE)
< >	not equal to	'A' < > 'B' (TRUE)
>	greater than	9.7 > 9 (TRUE)
<	less than	9.7 < 9 (FALSE)
> =	greater than or equal to	'B' > = 'A' (TRUE)
< =	less than or equal to	'A' < = 'A' (TRUE)

Boolean variables can be assigned values as a result of evaluating a Boolean expression:

```
HasOverdues := DueDate < TodaysDate;
```

In this statement the expression to the right of : = is checked. If the due date is less than the current date, the expression is true, and HasOverdues is assigned the value TRUE.

Boolean variables can be a useful way of saving the results of a condition checked in another part of the program, or of storing the user's answer to a question in an interactive program. In such cases it is important to give the Boolean variable a meaningful name. "Answer" or "result" are not particularly helpful; "HasCirculated" or "non_resident" can help the programmer recall the use for which the information was intended.

PRACTICE PROBLEM FOUR: NUMBER AND COST OF ACQUISITIONS

Our next problem provides practice with arithmetic operators and with counting. We want to read in prices of books and add them to a running total. We also want to count the number of prices we read, so we can divide the final total spent by the number of books purchased, and find the average price per book.

To be sure we begin with the running tally (the variable total) and the counter (num) at zero, we must "initialize" these variables to zero. This process of assigning a beginning value to a variable is important in computer programming—like finding a clean sheet of paper on which to begin your arithmetic or writing. If you do not initialize a variable you cannot be sure what its starting value will be, so it is wise to initialize the variable to the value you will want to use. To set total and num to zero:

```
total := 0;   num := 0;
```

You will need to decide on a maximum price for each book, which will be handled as a real variable, in order to format the output display. For the practice program count, the prices are allowed up to six spaces, including decimal point and minus sign.

A sample data file, COUNT.TXT, is:

```
9.95
10
0
-3
4.75
29.50
5.25
35.00
19.99
12.88
```

Notice that the data file does not use dollar signs in front of the prices, and that prices in whole dollars do not need to include the decimal point and subsequent zeroes. The file also includes an anomalous value of −3. This will be used to test the program, which is supposed to detect and ignore negative prices.

The progam COUNT.PAS, which reads the book prices, keeps a running total, and calculates that the average book price is:

```
PROGRAM count;
{ number and cost of acquisitions }
{$U+}
VAR fil: TEXT;
   filname: STRING[12];
   price, total: REAL;
   num: INTEGER;
BEGIN
WRITELN ('Type name of data file. e.g., count.txt');
READLN (filname);
ASSIGN (fil,filname);
RESET (fil);
   total:=0; num:=0;  (*initialize variables*)
   WHILE NOT EOF (fil) DO
   BEGIN
      READLN (fil,price);
      IF price < 0 THEN
         WRITELN ('Invalid data, price ',price:6:2, ' ignored.')
      ELSE BEGIN
         num:=num + 1;
         total:=total + price;
         END;
   END;
   WRITELN ('Total number of items is ', num);
   WRITELN ('Average cost per item is $', total/num:6:2);
END.
```

The IF-THEN-ELSE statement checks each price read to determine if it is less than zero. If so, an error notice is displayed. Otherwise num, the counter, is incremented (has one added to its value) and total becomes equal to its previous value plus the value of the variable price.

When the EOF condition is met, the total number of prices read is reported and the average price per item is calculated and reported. The last WRITELN statement is particularly interesting, because it shows results of an arithmetic operation, rather than a variable name, formatted for output. Here division is indicated by a slash (/), because one of the numbers involved is a real number and the result may have a fractional component.

The output displayed when this program is run:

```
Type name of data file, e.g., count.txt
count.txt
Invalid data, price  -3.00 ignored.
Total number of items is 9
Average cost per item is $ 14.15
```

In this example the average is calculated correctly. (The actual value of the average price, before rounding, is $14.14666.) Sometimes minor errors can occur if the general TURBO Pascal is used. There is a special version, TURBO-BCD (for Binary Coded Decimal), which provides greater accuracy in computations with real numbers. If your COUNT.PAS results and your own calculations are different by a small amount, this may be why.

7. Types and Constants

We have used variables as reserved spaces in computer memory to which different values, of specified types, may be assigned. Pascal also allows us to create new data types and to declare and use constants, names which can be used in place of the values assigned to them. These values do not change; they are "constant" throughout the program.

TYPE DECLARATION

TURBO Pascal provides character, string, text, integer, real, and Boolean data types. It is also possible to create one's own data types for handling special data. For example, we may wish to create a data type to be used for variables to represent the following borrower categories: freshman, sophomore, junior, senior. The type declaration is given in the declaration portion of the program and begins with the reserved word TYPE, followed by type definitions, each including the name of the type, the equals sign, the type, and a semicolon:

```
TYPE status = (freshman, sophomore, junior, senior);
```

This can be particularly valuable if a constant is used in several procedures within a program (see Chapter 9).

Constants are useful as short forms for large names or numbers that will be used frequently in a program; for example, the library's name will be printed on various recall and overdue notices. Constants also provide a convenient way to update programs; if the fine rate for overdues must be modified, only the constant declaration need be changed.

CONSTANT DECLARATION

The constant declaration begins with the reserved word CONST, followed by the name of the constant, an equals sign, then the value to be assigned to the constant, then a semicolon. This may be followed by additional constant declarations.

The constant declaration occurs in the declaration section of the program. It may be placed before or after the variable declaration (VAR).

If we wish to declare constants for faculty and student overdue fine rates and the library's name:

```
CONST  fac = 0.05;
       stu = 0.25;
       libname = 'Pleasant State University Library';
```

This declaration establishes a faculty fine rate, fac, of 5¢, and a student fine rate, stu, of 25¢.

USING CONSTANTS

When the value stored in a constant is needed in a program, use the name of the constant. To compute a faculty member's overdue fines, multiply the total days all items are overdue by the faculty fine rate:

```
total_days * fac
```

To include the library's name in the overdue notice, use the constant "libname":

```
WRITE (name, 'amount due ', libname,' $', fine);
```

PRACTICE PROBLEM FIVE: COMPUTING FINES

Write a program to calculate fines for overdue books. The input file should include the borrower's name (up to thirty spaces), the borrower's status (F for faculty, S for student), and the number of days each book is overdue. Status and days overdue are separated by blanks, and no record is more than one line in length. A sample data file, FINES.TXT, includes one erroneous status code (for A. Nobody):

```
Fred Smith                    F 3 6 8
Edith Johnson                 F 12 4 2
A. Nobody                     I 29 36 22 5
Roger Anderson                S 5 6
William Jones                 S 9 16 7
```

Your program (FINES.PAS) may use any fine rates you choose, but be sure to allow enough space for printing the total overdue fine in your output format. The output should start a new line for each borrower's name and total fine. You may wish to incorporate enhancements such as handling mistyped status codes and including the library name in the overdue notice.

This problem represents a component of an automated circulation system. Think about the following questions in this context:

How might the problem be defined to be more realistic?

What other components might you expect in an automated circulation system?

What would you need to consider to incorporate this overdue notice program into an automated circulation system?

What form might the input and output have in a real system?

COMPUTING FINES: PROGRAM AND ANALYSIS

The sample program FINES.PAS computes fines for two types of borrowers—faculty and students. It uses constants for the actual fine rates, and for the library name, which is displayed with the fine message.

There are two major parts to the processing. First the borrower's name and status are read, then a WHILE NOT EOLN (while not end of line) statement controls reading the number of days each book is overdue. As each number is read, it is added to the total days overdue. After all overdues are read for that borrower a READLN statement positions the file so that the next READ will be from the next patron record.

The second part of the processing is to compute fines and display the results. This begins with writing the borrower's name and the words "amount due Pleasant State University Library $." Then the fine is computed and displayed. The fine rate used depends on the borrower's status. If the status code is anything other than "F," the student fine rate is used. However, if the status is neither "F" nor "S" a notice is displayed.

```
PROGRAM fines;
{Compute fines--two classes of patrons, multiple overdues}
{$U+}
CONST fac = 0.05;
   stu = 0.25;
   libname = 'Pleasant University Library';
VAR fil: TEXT;
   filname: STRING[12];
   name: STRING[30];
   days, total_days: INTEGER;
   status: CHAR; {status code, F=faculty, S=student}
BEGIN
WRITELN ('Type name of data file, e.g., fines.txt');
READLN (filname);
ASSIGN (fil, filname);
RESET (fil);
   WHILE NOT EOF (fil) DO
   BEGIN
      total_days := 0; {initialize total}
      READ (fil, name, status);
      WHILE NOT EOLN (fil) DO
      BEGIN
         READ (fil, days);
         total_days  := total_days + days;
      END;
      READLN (fil); {move on to next record}
      WRITELN (name );
      WRITE ('     amount due ', libname, ' $');
      IF status='F' THEN WRITELN (total_days * fac:6:2)
      ELSE BEGIN
         WRITELN (total_days * stu:6:2);
         IF status <> 'S' THEN WRITELN
            ('    Invalid status code, student rate used');
      END;
   END;
END.
```

When FINES.PAS is run with the data file FINES.TXT, this is the result:

```
Type name of data file, e.g., fines.txt
fines.txt
Fred Smith
     amount due Pleasant University Library $  0.85
Edith Johnson
     amount due Pleasant University Library $  0.90
A. Nobody
     amount due Pleasant University Library $ 23.00
    Invalid status code, student rate used
Roger Anderson
     amount due Pleasant University Library $  2.75
William Jones
     amount due Pleasant University Library $  8.00
```

8. String Variables

Many library uses of computers involve working with character strings—sequences of letters, numbers, and other characters. In the official definition of Pascal, character string manipulation requires the creation of special routines or functions. TURBO Pascal, however, incorporates string handling functions and procedures, making it easier to write programs which process data files containing text.

STRING DECLARATION

A TURBO Pascal string is a sequence of characters. In declaring a string variable its name is followed by a colon, the reserved word STRING, then the string's maximum length, in square brackets. We have been using string variables of up to twelve characters to record the name of the data file in each practice program. Recall that part of the variable declaration:

```
VAR filname : STRING[12];
```

Strings may be from zero to 255 characters long. It is useful to remember that on most CRT terminals one line is eighty characters.

STRING ASSIGNMENT

Values are assigned to string variables as they are to other variables. Values may be read from an input file:

READLN (filname, variablename);

or assigned using the := operator. Be sure to use single quotation marks around a literal string being assigned to a string variable:

libname := 'Pleasant Public Library';

If a string is too long to fit into the string variable, only the leftmost characters of the string, up to the length of the string variable, will be used. In the case of libname, if it were defined to have a maximum length of twelve, the assignment would result in the content of libname being Pleasant Pub. If the string is shorter than the maximum length, the extra spaces are ignored.

TURBO Pascal provides several built-in functions and procedures for handling strings. These deal with length, position, deletion, insertion, copying, concatenation, and conversion between string and numeric values. (Functions and procedures in general are discussed in Chapter 9.)

LENGTH

The LENGTH function takes as its argument (or "works on") a string variable. It returns an integer, which is the number of characters in the string. If the string libname has the value "Pleasant Public Library" then the expression

LENGTH (libname):

returns the value 23. LENGTH is useful as a pointer to the end of a string, and it is often used with other string handling functions.

POSITION (POS)

The position function, POS, gives the position of the first occurrence of a specified value in a string. It has the format:

POS (<object>, <string>);

where <object> is the value to be found, and <string> is the string in which the <object> is sought. POS returns an integer, which is the place in the string where the first character of <object> occurs. Using the string libname, containing "Pleasant Public Library,"

```
POS (' ', libname);
```

we get the value 9, since the first blank is the ninth character in the string. The expression

```
POS ('Carnegie', libname);
```

returns the value 0, because the <object> does not occur in the <string>.

```
lib := POS ('Library', libname);
```

assigns the variable "lib" the value 17, the position of the first character of the <object> in the <string>.

DELETE

DELETE removes a specified number of characters from a string. You must specify the string, the position at which to start deleting, and the number of characters to be removed. It takes the form:

```
DELETE (<string>, <position>, <num>);
```

The character in the place indicated by <position> will be deleted. If the string "letters" contains 'ABCDEF' then

```
DELETE (letters, 3, 2);
```

will set "letters" equal to 'ABEF.' If <num> is larger than the length of the string, all characters after the <position> are deleted:

```
DELETE (letters, 3, 10);
```

gives the result "AB." If the <position> is larger than the length of the <string>, no characters are deleted.

If we wish to change the word "Library" in the string libname to the abbreviation "Lib," we need to delete the letters "rary." Using the variable lib, which contains the position of the first letter of "Library" in that string, we must move three characters to the right (to position lib + 3), and then delete four characters:

```
DELETE (libname, lib + 3, 4);
```

Now "Pleasant Public Lib" is stored in libname.

INSERT

The INSERT procedure places a character or string into a string at a specified position. INSERT has the format:

INSERT (<object>, <string>, <position>);

If "letters" contains 'ABCDEF' then

INSERT ('XYZ', letters, 2);

yields the string "letters" with the value 'AXYZBCDEF.' If the <position> is greater than the length of the <string>, the <object> is added to the end of the <string>. In the above case, with "letters" containing 'ABCDEF':

INSERT ('XYZ', letters, 15);

gives "letters" containing 'ABCDEFXYZ.' In cases in which the declared length of <string> is less than the new <string> with insertions, characters are truncated on the right; the leftmost characters, up to the length of <string>, are retained.

Returning to the abbreviation of "Library" in libname, if we wish to insert a period following the "Lib," we know it must be placed three spaces beyond the position indicated by the variable lib:

INSERT ('.', libname, lib + 3);

COPY

The COPY function extracts a number of characters, called a substring, from a string. The COPY format specifies the string from which to copy, the position at which to start copying, and the number of characters to copy:

variable := COPY (<string>, <position>, <num>);

If <position> is greater than the length of the <string>, the result is an empty, or null, string. If <num> added to <position> extends beyond the length of the <string>, only characters up to the end of <string> are given in the COPY.

COPY is frequently used to create a smaller string, skipping over part of a larger string. For instance, if we have a file from which we read the string "name," in the format:

lastname comma blank firstname

we can locate the firstname and COPY it to the variable "first":

```
place := POS (', ', name);

endpoint := LENGTH (name);

first := COPY (name, place + 2, endpoint);
```

This method of using the integer variables "place" and "endpoint" as pointers, to indicate locations in the string, is often helpful. It is possible to produce a more efficient program, though one which may be more difficult for humans to follow, by incorporating the calculation of the pointers in the COPY command. This means the variables "place" and "endpoint" do not have to be declared, nor are values assigned to these variables.

```
first := COPY (name, POS (',',name) + 2, LENGTH (name));
```

Using string functions within string functions is possible, but it can become complex!
(Question: Why was the pointer "endpoint" not named "end?")

CONCATENATION (CONCAT)

The concatenation function, CONCAT, chains together, or concatenates, two or more strings. The strings to be joined are separated by commas, and specified in the order in which they are to appear in the resulting string:

```
CONCAT (<string_1>, <string_2>);
```

TURBO Pascal also allows the + operator as a way of concatenating strings. The joining of strings one and two can also be accomplished by:

```
<string_1> + <string_2>
```

If we have a first name in the variable "first" and a last name in the variable "last," we can concatenate them, with a blank between, to produce the variable "name":

```
name := CONCAT (first, ' ', last);
```

"name" contains firstname blank lastname.

NUMERIC-TO-STRING CONVERSION (STR)

The STR procedure converts a numeric variable to a string value. For example, if we wish to insert commas to identify thousands, changing 19762 to 19,762, we must first change the integer to a string. The conversion procedure has the format:

```
STR (<num>, <string>);
```

where <num> is the numeric value and <string> the string variable in which the result is stored. To accomplish the conversion we use:

```
STR (number, charstr);
```

Now, to insert the comma:

```
INSERT (',', charstr, LENGTH (charstr) - 3);
```

STRING-TO-NUMERIC CONVERSION (VAL)

VAL converts a string variable to a numeric one, either integer or real. For this process TURBO Pascal uses an additional integer variable to indicate if the conversion was successful, or where the conversion failed. The format is:

```
VAL (<string>, <num>, <code>);
```

The string to be converted is <string>, and its numeric value is stored in the variable <num>. It will be an integer if <num> is declared an integer variable, real if <num> is real. The <code> must be a declared integer variable. If the conversion is successful <code> will be 0 on completion; otherwise the value of <num> will be undefined, and <code> will record the position in the <string> at which the conversion failed.

For example, if we have read the first character of a call number into the variable "dui," and wish to convert dui to an integer variable, "int" ("int" and "result" being integer variables):

```
VAL (dui, int, result);
```

If dui contains the character '3' int will have the value 3. If dui contains a non-numeric character, perhaps 'F' for a 'FIC' call number, the VAL conversion will leave int undefined, while result will be set to 1, indicating that the conversion failed at the first character of the string.

PRACTICE PROBLEM SIX: INVERTING NAMES

Write a program which will read authors' names in inverted order (lastname comma blank firstname) and print the names in the order firstname blank lastname. The input file should have one name per line. Names have up to thirty characters total; assume all thirty characters *could* be a "last" name (as in a corporate body's name). A sample data file, RENAME.TXT, is:

```
Davis, Charles H.
Lundeen, Gerald W.
Tenopir, Carol
Lancaster, F. Wilfrid
University of Illinois
Smith, Linda C.
Divilbiss, J. D.
Henderson, Kathryn Luther
Christo
```

The program RENAME.PAS reads in a name, and checks for the position of a comma. If there is no comma, the name is assumed to be in proper order, so the inversion commands are skipped and the name is accepted as read. If a comma is found, everything to the left of the comma is assigned to the variable "lastname." Everything from two places to the right of the comma (skipping over the comma and blank) is assigned to the variable "firstname." Then firstname, a literal blank, and lastname are concatenated and assigned to the variable "author."

```
PROGRAM rename;
{This program reads names in inverted order (last, first, middle) and
displays the names in first middle last order}
{$U+}
VAR fil: TEXT;
   filname: STRING[12];
   author, firstname, lastname: STRING[30];
   pointer: INTEGER;
BEGIN
WRITELN ('Type name of file to use, e.g. rename.txt');
READLN (filname);
ASSIGN (fil, filname);
RESET (fil);
WHILE NOT EOF (fil) DO
```

```
   BEGIN
   READLN (fil, author);
   pointer := pos (',', author);  {find comma after last name}
      IF pointer <> 0 THEN BEGIN  {pointer = 0 means name in one part,
                          skip inversion routine, leave author as read}
   lastname := COPY (author, 1, pointer-1);
   firstname := COPY (author, pointer+2, LENGTH (author));
                 {firstname is everything after comma and blank}
   author := CONCAT (firstname, ' ', lastname);
   END;  {end routine for inverting name}
   WRITELN (author);
END;  {end of block controlled by WHILE statement}
WRITELN;  WRITELN ('Names inverted');
END.
```

When the program is run, using the data file RENAME.TXT, the output is :

```
Type name of file to use, e.g. rename.txt
rename.txt
Charles H. Davis
Gerald W. Lundeen
Carol Tenopir
F. Wilfrid Lancaster
University of Illinois
Linda C. Smith
J. D. Divilbiss
Kathryn Luther Henderson
Christo

Names inverted

>
```

9. Program Structure

There are occasions when a set of instructions is needed at several points within a computer program. For example, a circulation program may check to see if an item is overdue when it is returned, when it is renewed, or when a patron asks to borrow it. Whereas it would be possible to repeat the instructions for checking an item's status at each of these points of potential use in the program, it is easier to handle that set of operations as a separate unit of the program. When the need to check an item's status arises, this separate unit, or subprogram, is executed. The flow of program control is transferred to the appropriate subprogam when it is "called" or "invoked," and control returns to the calling portion of the program after the subprogram is executed.

This approach to creating subprograms allows programmers to divide a complex set of operations into smaller, more manageable pieces. Working with subprograms to accomplish parts of the overall objective is a way to focus attention on a specific area. Chapter 11 describes using this approach to writing a computer program.

Pascal provides two kinds of subprograms: functions and procedures. Functions operate with zero or more program variables to produce specified results. Procedures can be more flexible; they often involve lengthier and more complex operations. In addition, functions and procedures use different syntax. Functions are used in expressions in which they return a single value; procedures are written as separate statements.

FUNCTIONS

In the previous chapter TURBO Pascal's string handling functions were described. A function is a portion of program code that takes some values (called arguments or parameters), performs some operation on the arguments, and returns an output value. A function can be thought of as a box into which you put one or more values, and out of which you get one value. The CONCAT function, for example, is called (or invoked) by giving the function name and two arguments: the strings to be joined (see Figure 3).

Standard Pascal has several built-in functions, mostly for numeric computation. TURBO Pascal provides additional built-in functions. Beyond those for string handling, TURBO's UpCase (convert a letter to upper case), Random (random number generator) and KeyPressed (check if a response has been typed at the keyboard) can be particularly helpful in some library applications. The TURBO Pascal manual provides descriptions of these and other functions.

Programmers can create additional functions in Pascal. Function definitions should be placed immediately after the variable declaration portion of the program, so that the function is known before it is invoked, or used, in the program. The function declaration has the format:

```
FUNCTION FunctionName (arg_1:argtype_1, arg_2:argtype_2, . . .
    arg_n:argtype_n):function_type;
  [type, constant, variable declarations]
  BEGIN
    [operations, assigning a value to FunctionName]
  END;
```

For functions that do not need arguments from the calling program, the arguments and parentheses may be omitted. If arguments are used, each must have its type specified in the function heading. Following this list of arguments and their types in parentheses, the type of the function is given. The function type tells the kind of value the function will return to its caller. The type may be integer, real, Boolean, or character, or a programmer-defined type. If the function receives arguments of a user-defined type, or if the function type is user-defined, this type definition must be given in a declaration outside the function. Following the function heading, before the BEGIN, any types, constants, or variables to be used only within the function are declared in standard declaration statements. If no function-specific types, constants, or variables are needed, these declarations are omitted.

As an example, consider a function that uses TURBO Pascal's UpCase

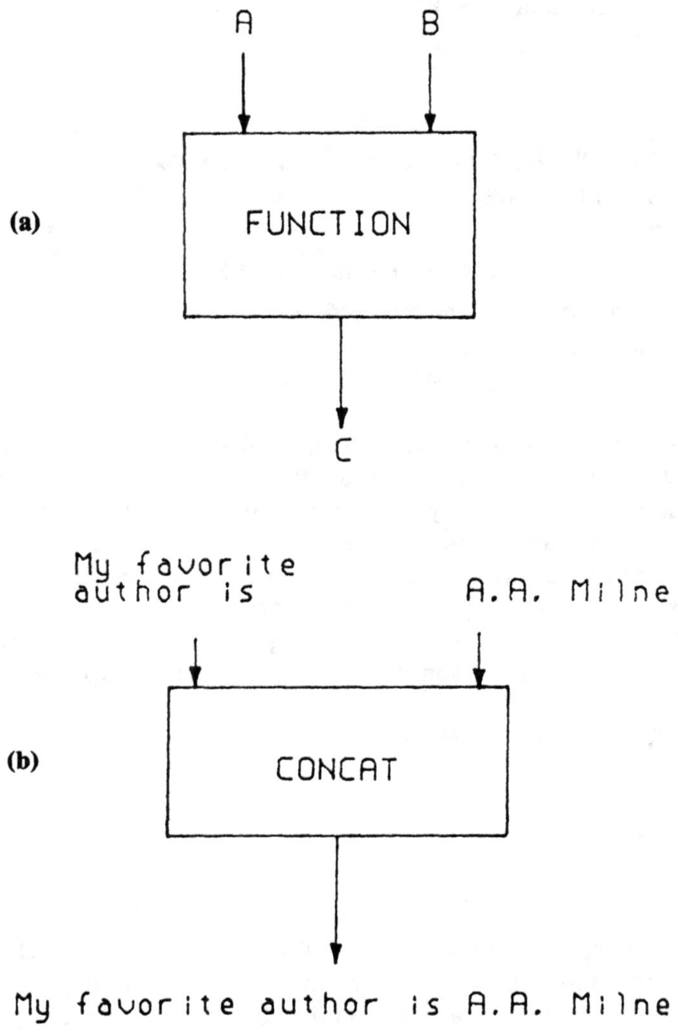

Figure 3
(a) Function Diagram; (b) Concatenation Function

function to convert a character string to upper case letters. This function is of a programmer-defined type, KeyString, a string of length 30:

```
TYPE: KeyString = STRING[30];
.
.
.
FUNCTION Upper (instring: KeyString): KeyString;
  VAR i: INTEGER;
  BEGIN
    FOR i := 1 TO LENGTH (instring) DO
      instring[i] := UpCase (instring[i]);
    upper := instring;
  END; {function upper}
```

The function is named "upper." Its argument is "instring," a KeyString (up to 30 characters) and it returns another KeyString. The integer variable "i" is declared; it exists only within the function. The function uses a FOR loop to convert each character of instring to upper case, then assigns the new version of instring to upper. This function will be called from one or more other points in the program. For example, one might wish to convert two names to upper case before comparing them to see if they are the same. The result of the comparison is stored in the Boolean variable "match."

```
match := upper (name1) = upper (name2);
```

PROCEDURES

A procedure is like a function in that it is a distinct part of a larger program. A procedure performs a set of operations to accomplish a specific task. A procedure is not required to have arguments (although it may), nor does it return a value. As a result, a procedure does not have a type as part of its declaration. The procedure declaration begins with the reserved word PROCEDURE and has the form:

```
PROCEDURE ProcedureName (formal parameter list);
  [types, constants, variables declarations]
  BEGIN
    [statements to perform procedure operations]
  END;
```

Type, constant, and variable declarations are given for procedure-specific types, contants, or variables, called local types, constants, or variables. Variables in the formal parameter list represent variables in the calling program that are "passed as parameters" to the procedure. Procedures may operate on variables in the calling program, even if they are not passed as parameters; these are called global variables. However, if a variable is used only within a procedure, it is wise to handle it as a local variable. A local variable is declared and exists only within a given procedure. This reduces the chances of producing unwanted side effects and makes it easier to use the procedure in several programs without modifying each program's declaration section to include procedure-specific variables.

The formal parameter list in the procedure heading gives the names to be used for the parameters passed to the procedure when it is called. A Pascal procedure can deal with values passed to it from outside the procedure (the actual parameters) in one of two ways illustrated in Illustration 9.2:

(1) The formal parameters' values can be modified within the procedure without affecting the values of the actual parameters. This approach, termed "call by value," protects the values of actual parameters, which is often desirable, but it limits the ability of the procedure to interact with the rest of the program. The formal parameter list for this approach has the form:

```
(parameter_1: type_1; parameter_2: type_2);
```

(2) Modification of formal parameters' values within the procedure can produce corresponding changes in the values of the actual parameters. This approach, termed "call by reference," increases the effect of the procedure on the program as a whole and also saves storage space in the computer's memory because the parameters need not be copied for use in the procedure. The formal parameter list in the procedure declaration is:

```
(VAR parameter_1: type_1; VAR parameter_2: type_2);
```

If parameters are of the same type they may be listed, separated by commas, with the ": type" following the list. Types may be integer, real, Boolean, character, string, or a programmer-defined type.

Procedures must be defined before they are used in a program. For relatively simple programs it is advisable to place procedure definitions after the variable declaration and functions definitions (if any) of the main program. Since one function or procedure may invoke another, the sequence in which they are written in the program can be significant. Functions or procedures used by others must be declared before they are invoked. Program Comparer uses a procedure and a function to perform a comparison of two strings.

```
PROGRAM PassByValue (INPUT, OUTPUT);
{Demonstrate Pass by Value - procedure variables}

TYPE word = STRING[4];
VAR main_one:word;

   PROCEDURE HelpMe (proc_one:word);
   BEGIN {procedure HelpMe}
     proc_one := 'HELP';
   END; {procedure HelpMe}

BEGIN {main program}
   main_one := 'OK';
   HelpMe (main_one);
   WRITELN ('main_one = ', main_one);
END. {main program}
```

output: OK

1. Pass by value: proc_one is assigned a value within the procedure, but its value in the outside program is not affected by this assignment.

```
PROGRAM PassByReference (INPUT, OUTPUT);
{Demonstrate Pass by Reference - procedure variables}

TYPE word = STRING[4];
VAR main_one:word;

   PROCEDURE HelpMe (VAR proc_one:word);
   BEGIN {procedure HelpMe}
     proc_one := 'HELP';
   END; {procedure HelpMe}

BEGIN {main program}
   main_one := 'OK';
   HelpMe (main_one);
   WRITELN ('main_one = ', main_one);
END. {main program}
```

output: HELP

2. Pass by reference: proc_one is assigned as value within the procedure, this value is retained when control returns to the outside program.

```
PROGRAM comparer;
{use procedure and function to compare 2 words}
TYPE KeyString = STRING[30];
VAR first, second: KeyString;


FUNCTION upper (instring: KeyString): KeyString;
   VAR i: INTEGER;
   BEGIN
      FOR i := 1 TO LENGTH (instring) DO
         instring[i] := UpCase (instring[i]);
      upper := instring;
   END; {function upper}


PROCEDURE compare (VAR word1, word2: KeyString);
   BEGIN
      word1 := upper (word1);
      word2 := upper (word2);
      IF word1 = word2 THEN
         WRITELN (word1,' and ', word2,' are the same.')
         ELSE WRITELN ('The words are not the same.');
   END; {procedure compare}


BEGIN {main program}
   WRITELN ('Enter first word'); READLN (first);
   WRITELN ('Enter second word'); READLN (second);
   compare (first, second);
   WRITELN (first, ', ', second);
END. {main program}
```

The main program reads two variables named "first" and "second," the two strings to be compared. It then invokes the procedure compare, simply by using the procedure name as a statement. First and second are the actual parameters passed to the procedure. "Compare" uses call by reference for its formal parameters, word1 and word2. Changes made to word1 in the procedure are made to the variable first; similarly changes to word2 are reflected in the main program variable second. Function upper is called from the procedure "compare." Each word is converted to all uppercase letters, and the uppercase form is preserved. After this conversion the two words are compared. When control is returned to the main program first and second are printed. This allows the programmer to verify that first and second were converted to upper case. An example of comparer's execution is:

```
Enter first word
little
Enter second word
small
The words are not the same.
LITTLE, SMALL

>

Enter first word
mcConnell
Enter second word
Mcconnell
MCCONNELL and MCCONNELL are the same.
MCCONNELL, MCCONNELL

>
```

10. Arrays

Often we need to process large groups of data items of a given type, or to use a series of values more than once. If we need to work with 100 values, for example to put 100 call numbers in shelf list order, we could declare 100 variables with the same attributes, then assign the call numbers to these variables. While this approach is possible, it rapidly becomes cumbersome. In addition, if we need to refer to all the call numbers as a group we have no way to do so.

In Pascal operations on groups of similar data, elements are facilitated by storing the data in "arrays." An array is an indexed list in which all the elements have the same attributes (variable type, and size, for string variables). Arrays may be elements of other arrays, forming multidimensional arrays.

ARRAY DECLARATION

Arrays of variables are defined in the variable declaration part of the program. The declaration gives the array name, a colon, the reserved word ARRAY, followed without any blanks by the array index values, enclosed in square brackets, then the reserved word "of" and the type of variables to be stored in the array. For example:

```
VAR class : ARRAY[0..9] OF INTEGER;
```

sets up an array, or list, called "class." There are ten elements in the array, labeled 0 through (. .) 9. Each element of the array is an integer. We may visualize the array class as a sequence of labeled compartments; all compartments are alike, and will be used to store integer values. The label for each compartment is an integer from 0 to 9:

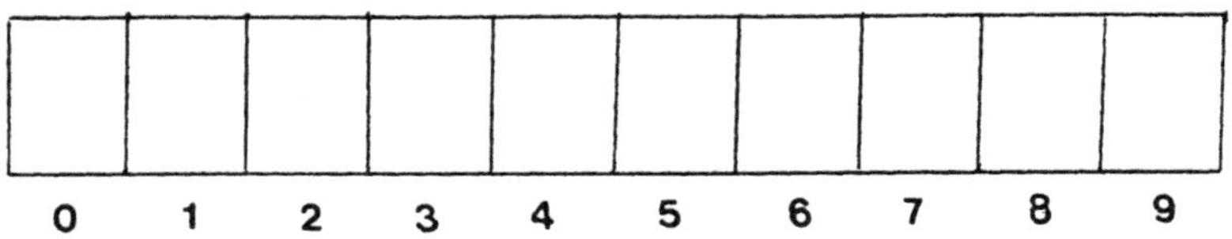

An array may be indexed by integers (as is "class") or by byte, Boolean, character values, or user-defined ordinal types. Integer and character indices are most common. If a character index is used, the labels must be in single quotation marks:

```
VAR class2 : ARRAY['0'..'9'] OF INTEGER;
```

An array may be indexed by negative numbers:

```
VAR avg_temp : ARRAY[-20..40] OF REAL; {degrees Celsius}
```

Arrays composed of strings are useful in library applications.

```
VAR shelf_list : ARRAY[1..200] OF STRING[20];
```

may be used to work with a file of up to 200 call numbers.

A two-dimensional array can be envisioned as a table, with rows and columns. As an example of handling information on authors' names, we may group the names by initial letter, then process the group beginning with each letter. If we assume there will be no more than ten names beginning with the same letter, we can use a two-dimensional array with twenty-six columns (one for each letter) and ten rows (one for each potential author in each letter column). We can use letters to label the columns, numbers for the rows. The declaration separates the two indices with a comma:

```
VAR names : ARRAY['A'..'Z', 1..10] OF STRING[30];
```

This reserves 260 memory locations, each of which may contain strings of up to thirty characters:

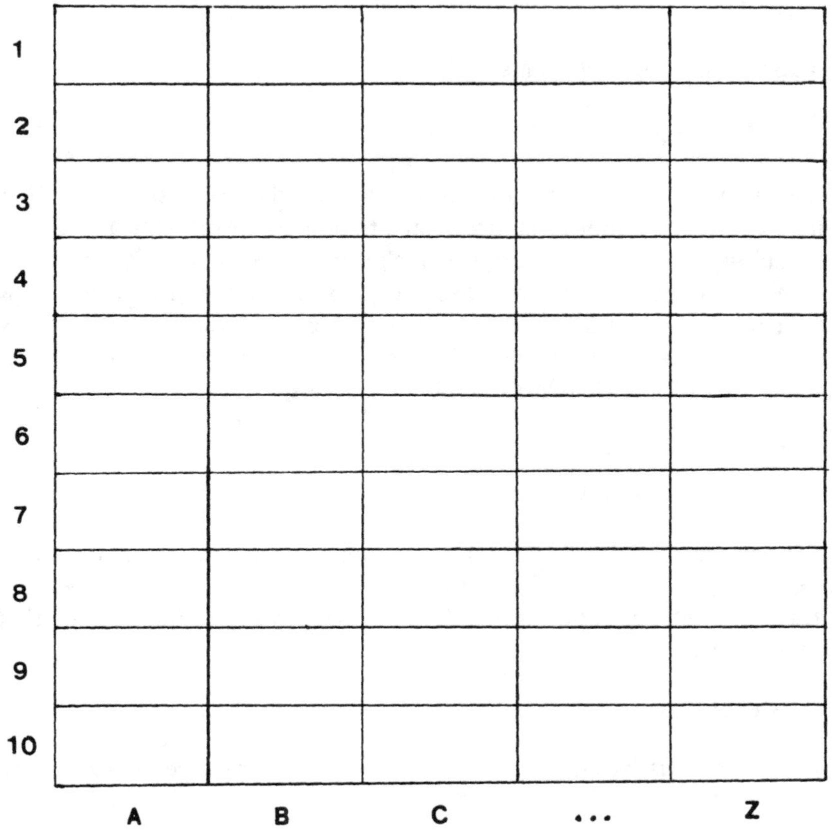

Although array declarations are brief, the amount of computer memory they consume can be large. Be particularly careful with multidimensional arrays, in which the total number of variables in an array is the product of the numbers of elements specified by each index.

VAR big : ARRAY[1..50, 1..50, 1..50] OF INTEGER;

reserves an array of 125,000 memory locations.

USING ARRAYS

Individual elements of an array are referred to by the array name followed by the index of the element in square brackets (no spaces). For array "class," a one-dimensional array with index 0 . .9, we refer to the first element as:

```
class[0]
```

To add the first three elements:

```
total := class[0] + class[1] + class[2]
```

The index value in square brackets is termed the array subscript. It is certainly possible, although cumbersome, to add all the elements in "class" by specifying the unique subscript of each element. Such an effort becomes even more onerous for larger arrays. For this reason we often use a FOR statement to control work with an array. The control variable in the FOR statement can also serve as the array index. If we have an integer variable, "i," we can add the elements of "class" this way:

```
FOR i := 0 TO 9 DO
  total := total + class[i];
```

The subscript for an element of a two-dimensional array must give both index values, i.e., must specify both column and row. To refer to the array "names," which has columns A to Z and rows 1 to 10, we indicate the first name in row C:

```
names['C',1]
```

If we wish to initialize all elements of "names" to blanks, we can use a FOR statement within a FOR statement:

```
FOR a := 'A' TO 'Z' DO
  FOR i := 1 TO 10 DO
    names[a,i] := ' ';
```

The first FOR statement uses the character variable "a" to process one column at a time. The second FOR statement identifies each row in turn.

PRACTICE PROBLEM SEVEN: CIRCULATION TALLY

This practice problem uses arrays, and also provides experience with numeric variables and arithmetic calculation. We are to read a data file of book records. Each record represents one circulation transaction. We are to count the number of books which circulated in each class, using the first summary of the Dewey Decimal Classification (ten classes only—using the first digit of the call number). We will also calculate the percentage of the total circulation represented by each class, and print the results. A sample data file, CIRC.TXT is presented here:

```
546.03      THOMPSON              1969
822.912     JONES                 1930
543.26      SMITH                 1943
328.99      WILLIAMS              1974
418.5       JOHNSON               1976
612.54      PETERSON              1982
```

CIRCULATION TALLY: PROGRAM AND ANALYSIS

Circulation tally is a good example of using an array to process groups of the same kind of variable. The basic operation is that of counting, as we did in practice problem four, number and cost of acquisitions. Here we have an array of ten counters, instead of one, and we increment the appropriate one of the counters each time we process a circulation record. The selection of which counter to increment is based on the first character of the Dewey number. However, if we choose to use integers to index the array, we must use VAL to convert the character to an integer value. The program CIRC.PAS, which accomplishes this task, is:

```
PROGRAM circ;
{ number and percent of books circulated by first summary of Dewey }
{$U+}
VAR fil: TEXT;
    filname: STRING[12];
    dui: CHAR;
    class: ARRAY[0..9] OF INTEGER;
    num, ptr, result: INTEGER;
 BEGIN
 WRITELN ('Type name of data file, e.g., circ.txt');
 READLN (filname);
 ASSIGN (fil, filname);
 RESET (fil);
 FOR ptr := 0 TO 9 DO class[ptr] := 0; {initialize class to 0}
 num := 0;
    WHILE NOT EOF (fil) DO
    BEGIN
       READLN (fil,dui); {read first character, skip rest of line}
       VAL (dui, ptr, result);  {convert dui to integer}
       class[ptr] := class[ptr] + 1;
       num := num + 1;
    END;
    FOR ptr := 0 TO 9 DO
    BEGIN
       WRITE ('Dewey class ', ptr, ' circ = ', class[ptr]);
       WRITELN ('       percent of total circ = ',
          (class[ptr]/num * 100):6:2, '%');
    END;
    WRITELN ('Total items circulated = ', num);
END.
```

The output display from CIRC.PAS using data file CIRC.TXT is shown below:

```
Type name of data file, e.g., circ.txt
circ.txt
Dewey class 0 circ = 0       percent of total circ =   0.00%
Dewey class 1 circ = 0       percent of total circ =   0.00%
Dewey class 2 circ = 0       percent of total circ =   0.00%
Dewey class 3 circ = 1       percent of total circ =  16.67%
Dewey class 4 circ = 1       percent of total circ =  16.67%
Dewey class 5 circ = 2       percent of total circ =  33.33%
Dewey class 6 circ = 1       percent of total circ =  16.67%
Dewey class 7 circ = 0       percent of total circ =   0.00%
Dewey class 8 circ = 1       percent of total circ =  16.67%
Dewey class 9 circ = 0       percent of total circ =   0.00%
Total items circulated = 6
```

11. Program Writing Techniques, Testing, and Documentation

As we write programs to accomplish more and different tasks, the programs tend to become both longer and more complex. Computer scientists are working on ways to prove that programs are correct and will always perform as their designers intend. While we await programs that can prove programs correct, there are several aspects to the "art" of computer programming that help the human programmer develop clearly organized programs which are easier to analyze when problems arise.

In earlier programs we incorporated several techniques to help clarify programs. These include:

Choice of identifier names: Choosing names for variables and constants which reflect the values they will contain. "Dui" for the first character of the Dewey classification number or "last_name" for an author's last name are examples of meaningful variable names. Had we termed these variables "x" or "Aunt_Ada," for instance, the task of remembering what values they were to handle would be more difficult.

Format of program statements: Using blank space, including indentations, to make the program structure clear. While Pascal places no restrictions on the physical format of the program, except that statements are executed in the order that they are written, we have followed the general rules of writing one command per line, and indenting statements that are within a BEGIN-END block or subordinate to other statements—those controlled by a conditional statement, for example.

Use of comments: Employing informative comments that explain what is to be accomplished by the Pascal commands. Helpful comments summarize the actions to be performed in a function, procedure, or other complex part of a program. Use coments to enhance the reader's (or programmer's) understanding, not simply to translate a Pascal statement into English. For example, the following comment is uninformative:

```
READLN (fil, author); {read author from input file}
```

The comment does not provide any additional information to anyone who understands Pascal, and it would be better to omit the comment.

Defensive programming: Occasionally the data for a program do not meet the expectations of the programmer. Catching and handling such input errors improves programs. We used defensive programming in the fines program, when an invalid user status code caused an error message to be displayed. The more numerous the users of a program, the more important defensive programming becomes.

All of these techniques help to make programs easier to read and understand, and also help to reduce the chances of making mistakes. We will use comments to help structure the program in practice problem eight.

PRACTICE PROBLEM EIGHT: SDI USING DEWEY AND FICTION CODES

Selective dissemination of information (SDI) is a current awareness service for alerting library patrons to new items that meet their stated interests. The service can be performed manually, but now is usually computerized. SDI is most commonly offered by special libraries, but is finding wider application, sometimes through online retrieval services.

Patron interests are formulated as a "profile," typically using index terms, author names, and other parts of machine-readable bibliographic records and combining them by means of the Boolean operators AND, OR, NOT.

A simpler approach is to use the Dewey classification scheme for profile formulation and matching. This approach might be used in a public library, where a more general approach is often useful.

In our problem we use the first digit of the Dewey number to indicate subjects of interest, and a colon (:) to code for fiction. We need a two-dimensional array to store our book records and a one-dimensional array for counting the number in each class.

Write a program that will store, in the computer's main memory, information about books by the first summary of the Dewey schedule (by the first digit of the Dewey number) or by the fiction code, ":". Assume that there are no more than ten books in any one category. Once the book records have been stored, patron profiles will be read and book records matching each patron's profile printed in appropriate format with labels for each category. (Headings for each category will have to be stored in order to label the output.) Each patron's output should be headed with the patron's name and address, and separated from the previous patron's output by a blank line.

You will need three data files: first, the category headings, in order; second, the book records; and finally, the patron records, consisting of name, address, and codes for the areas of interest. We will use a colon as the fiction code, since it follows the character '9' in the machine representation. This allows us to use arrays of eleven elements, labeled '0' to ':' in the SDI program.

The data files for this program are:
HEAD.TXT— the list of headings, in order by Dewey class number. These will be used to label the book lists for each patron.

```
GENERAL
PHILOSOPHY
RELIGION
SOCIAL SCIENCE
PHILOLOGY
SCIENCE
TECHNOLOGY
FINE ARTS
LITERATURE
HISTORY
FICTION
```

BOOKS.TXT—containing the call number, author's last name, title, and publication data for each book. Fiction call numbers begin with a colon. Each record is one line, with the call numbers beginning in column one.

```
542.8     Smith     College chemistry                     1974
325.67    Adams     The welfare system                    1973
904.68    Johnson   History of Douglas County             1923
:FIC      Brown     Fear of frying                        1986
523.632   Randall   Quantitative analysis made simple     1978
246.8     Carter    Collected sermons                     1980
957.7     Gray      The Lahaina whale industry            1933
641.13    Barnard   Surgery for left-handers              1984
:FIC      Christy   Who done it?                          1990
:FIC      Spade     Not me                                1990
```

PATRON.TXT, giving the patron name, address, and number of interest areas on one line, and the interest categories on the next. Interest in fiction is coded with a colon.

```
Sam Smith            123 Main Street                      Urbana, IL 61801     3
56:
Ed Ho                4310 Ala Wai                         Honolulu, HI 96816   3
39:
Mary Jones           4300 Broad Street                    Champaign, IL 61820  4
1234
```

SDI: PROGRAM AND ANALYSIS

Before we begin writing Pascal commands for the SDI program, we should understand the problem and develop an outline for the steps to be performed. This outline can be written as a sequence of Pascal comments, forming the skeleton on which the program can be developed. To summarize the problem statement, the basic steps in the SDI program are:

{read headings for subject categories into headings array}

{read book records into books array, count books in each class}

{read patron record, print subject heading and books for each interest code}

Once we have declared the variables needed for this program, we can write the Pascal commands to accomplish each of these steps.

```
PROGRAM sdi;
{selective dissemination of information using dewey, fiction codes }
{$U+}
VAR fil: TEXT;
   filname: STRING[12];
   dui: CHAR;
   headings: ARRAY['0'..':'] OF STRING[14];
   count: ARRAY['0'..':'] OF INTEGER;
   line, patron: STRING[79];
   books: ARRAY['0'..':',1..10] OF STRING[79];
   counter, interests, num: INTEGER;

BEGIN
{ read headings for subject categories into headings array }
WRITELN (' Type name of headings data file, e.g., head.txt');
READLN (filname);
ASSIGN (fil, filname);
RESET (fil);
FOR dui := '0' TO ':' DO READLN (fil,headings[dui]);

{ read book records into books array, count books in each class }
WRITELN (' Type name of books data file, e.g., books.txt');
READLN (filname);
ASSIGN (fil, filname);
RESET (fil);
FOR dui:= '0' TO ':' DO count[dui]:= 0;
WHILE NOT EOF (fil) DO
BEGIN
   READLN (fil,line);
   dui := COPY (line,1,1);
   count[dui] := count[dui] + 1;
   books[dui,count[dui]] := line;
END;
```

```
{ read patron record, print subject heading and books for each interest code }
WRITELN (' Type name of patrons data file, e.g., patron.txt');
READLN (filname);
ASSIGN (fil, filname);
RESET (fil);
WHILE NOT EOF (fil) DO
BEGIN
   READLN (fil,patron, interests);
   WRITELN (patron);
   { get dui class from profile, print items from those classes }
   FOR num := 1 TO interests DO
   BEGIN
      READ (fil,dui);
      IF count[dui] > 0 THEN { at least one item in this class }
      BEGIN
         WRITELN (headings[dui]);
         FOR counter := 1 to count[dui] DO WRITELN (books[dui,counter]);
      END;
   END;
   READLN (fil);  { get to next patron record }
   WRITELN; { blank line before next patron's output }
 END;
 END.
```

Running SDI.PAS with the three data files listed above produces the following output:

```
Sam Smith            123 Main Street                         Urbana, IL 61801
SCIENCE
542.8        Smith        College chemistry                                  1974
523.632      Randall      Quantitative analysis made simple                  1978
TECHNOLOGY
641.13       Barnard      Surgery for left-handers                           1984
FICTION
:FIC         Brown        Fear of frying                                     1986
:FIC         Christy      Who done it?                                       1990
:FIC         Spade        Not me                                             1990

Ed Ho                4310 Ala Wai                            Honolulu, HI 96816
SOCIAL SCIENCE
325.67       Adams        The welfare system                                 1973
HISTORY
904.68       Johnson      History of Douglas County                          1923
957.7        Gray         The Lahaina whale industry                         1933
FICTION
:FIC         Brown        Fear of frying                                     1986
:FIC         Christy      Who done it?                                       1990
:FIC         Spade        Not me                                             1990

Mary Jones           4300 Broad Street                       Champaign, IL 61820
RELIGION
246.8        Carter       Collected sermons                                  1980
SOCIAL SCIENCE
325.67       Adams        The welfare system                                 1973
```

Note that REWRITE is used with output files in a manner similar to RESET with input files. CLOSE inserts an end-of-file mark, and is unique to output files.

PROCEDURES IN PROGRAM STRUCTURING

We can make the separate modules of a program more distinct by writing each as a procedure. We can rewrite the SDI program to use procedures for the three major tasks. Remember that each procedure must be defined in the program before it is invoked. The outline is:

```
PROCEDURE readcategories;
PROCEDURE readbooks;
PROCEDURE writenotices;
{Main program}
  readcategories;
  readbooks;
  writenotices;
```

Each procedure is called, or invoked, simply by giving the procedure name as a statement.

```
PROGRAM sdi;
{selective dissemination of information using dewey, fiction codes
 and procedures, writing to output file SDINOTICES.DAT }
{$U+}
VAR fil, outfil: TEXT;
   filname: STRING[12];
   dui: CHAR;
   headings: ARRAY['0'..':'] OF STRING[14];
   count: ARRAY['0'..':'] OF INTEGER;
   line: STRING[79];
   books: ARRAY['0'..':',1..10] OF STRING[79];

PROCEDURE readcategories; {read headings for subject categories}
BEGIN
   WRITELN (' Type name of headings data file, e.g., head.txt');
   READLN (filname); ASSIGN (fil, filname); RESET (fil);
   FOR dui := '0' TO ':' DO READLN (fil,headings[dui]);
END;

PROCEDURE readbooks; {read book records, count books in each class}
BEGIN
   WRITELN (' Type name of books data file, e.g., books.txt');
   READLN (filname); ASSIGN (fil, filname); RESET (fil);
   FOR dui:= '0' TO ':' DO count[dui]:= 0;
   WHILE NOT EOF (fil) DO
   BEGIN
      READLN (fil,line);
      dui := COPY (line,1,1);
      count[dui] := count[dui] + 1;
      books[dui,count[dui]] := line;
   END;
END;
```

```
PROCEDURE writenotices;
{ read patron record, print subject heading and books for each interest code }
VAR counter, interests, num: INTEGER;
   outfil: TEXT;
BEGIN
   ASSIGN (outfil, 'SDINOTICES.DAT'); REWRITE (outfil); {prepare output file }
   WRITELN ('Type name of patron file, e.g., patron.txt');
   READLN (filname); ASSIGN (fil, filname); RESET (fil);
   WHILE NOT EOF (fil) DO
   BEGIN
      READLN (fil, line, interests);
      WRITELN (outfil, line);
      { get dui class from profile, print items from those classes }
      FOR num := 1 TO interests DO
      BEGIN
         READ (fil,dui);
         IF count[dui] > 0 THEN { at least one item in this class }
         BEGIN
            WRITELN (outfil, headings[dui]);
            FOR counter := 1 to count[dui] DO
               WRITELN (outfil, books[dui,counter]);
         END;
      END;
      READLN (fil);  { get to next patron record }
      WRITELN (outfil); { blank line before next patron's output }
   END;
   CLOSE (outfil);
END;

BEGIN  { main program }
   readcategories;
   readbooks;
   writenotices;
END.
```

PROGRAM STRUCTURE AND DESIGN

As programs become longer and more complex, consideration of the overall program structure becomes more important. A clearly organized program does not "just happen," and the imposition of structure on a carelessly written program is a frustrating task. Good programming practice, what is known as "structured programming," stresses a modular approach. Our comment outline and procedures versions of the SDI program are examples of this approach.

We have discussed such matters as judicious choice of identifier names, formatting of program statements (such as indenting BEGIN-END blocks), the use of comments, and defensive programming (checking to assure that input data are valid and reasonable). These kinds of ideas help to make programs easier to read and understand, and also help to reduce the chances of making mistakes. We have also seen the three control logic structures (sequence, selection, and iteration) with which we are to construct our programs.

Let's look at what is involved in solving a programming problem.

1. First, you must understand the problem. This may seem obvious, but it is surprising how often people start writing program statements before they understand exactly what they want their programs to do.

Essential to this understanding are the two questions: What do I have to work with? (What is the input?) and: What do I want done with it? (What is the output?). When you understand the problem, state it as clearly and explicitly as possible in English (or some other natural language) or some combination of natural language and mathematics.

2. Divide the problem into a collection of smaller subproblems. At this level pay particular attention to the relationships of the subproblems to each other (e.g., are they to be executed sequentially or are some modules executed selectively, as for instance an error routine that will be performed only if bad data are encountered?). Programming statements to control the flow or communication between modules might be written at this level, with comments serving to indicate what each module will do.

3. Repeat step two with each module until the resulting comments are specific enough to make translation into program statements a relatively straightforward process.

Very often, at least some modules will end up being algorithms that you have used before. This happens more after you have been programming for a while, of course.

At some point in this process, an overall algorithm or solution to the problem will have to emerge. Just exactly how and when is hard to say. Experience helps, as does reading a variety of good programs.

This scheme is meant to indicate the basic approach and should not be considered a rigid formula. At any one stage in the process, ideas are likely to occur to you that affect other stages. For example, writing program statements may give you some new insight into problems that you thought you understood well. In actual practice there will be some jumping back and forth, restarting and backtracking. Solving problems is a creative act, and the creative part is virtually impossible to prescribe. What we can do is try to make the products of our creativity as orderly and as clear as possible. This helps in the creative process itself, since most problems of more than trivial size are solved in stages. It also helps in finding the nearly inevitable bugs in a program and makes for programs that are more readily modified and easier to understand.

Properly done, with the use of the three control logic units, the program should consist of a sequence of segments or modules, each of which performs some well-defined task. Such a program can be read without skipping all over the listing, and when properly formatted the logical structure should be clearly exhibited.

PROGRAM TESTING AND DEBUGGING

All of the above suggestions for the production of clearly thought-out, developed, structured, and formatted programs should greatly enhance your chances of writing a program that will actually do what it is supposed to do. Rarely will your program work on the first try; even if it seems to work initially, you need to assure yourself that it will work properly with a variety of data.

The compiler helps us with certain types of error detection. Syntax errors are found during the compilation, and error messages are displayed if you included the TURBO error messages when you began the programming session. Compiler error messages generally indicate approximately where an error occurs. It is wise to check the lines just before the error indicator, however, because a forgotten semicolon or misspelled word on the previous line may have caused the error.

Even if your program runs without error messages, it may be incorrect. You should check the output to see that the results are in fact what they should be. Checking usually means using a small set of test data for which you can generate the answers manually. In checking programs you should try to think of possible difficult values for data and try these.

Not only should the program give correct results for all possible valid data values, but it should cope with all possible invalid data as well. It is generally very difficult, if not impossible, to demonstrate that this ideal has been achieved.

We can classify errors into four types:

1. Errors in understanding the problem
2. Errors in understanding the programming language—syntax errors
3. Faulty algorithms—logical errors
4. Accidents—typographical errors and the like.

If your program compiles without errors but does not produce the correct output when run, it is time to "debug" the program—to find and remove programming errors, called "bugs" in the jargon of the field. Often the first step in debugging is to "play computer." You, the programmer, trace the execution of the program, working through what happens at each step, what is read from data files, what is stored in each variable, what data comparisons and manipulations are performed, and what is displayed with each WRITE statement.

Another debugging approach is to check to see what is contained in one or more variables at critical points in the program. WRITE statements can be inserted, then removed once the proper functioning of a portion of the program is ascertained. For example, if part of a program redefines the variable "name" to include whatever is to the right of the comma and blank in the variable, we may check to see that the command was executed properly by inserting a WRITELN statement, to display the previous and subsequent values of "name":

```
WRITELN ('name= ', name);
name := COPY (name, comma + 2, LENGTH (name));
WRITELN ('name= ', name);
```

Yet another tool for debugging is to "comment out" a part of the program. This includes putting comment symbols— { } or (* *) —around one or more statements. Those statements will be skipped during compilation and execution. If the program works properly (although not actually performing the functions commented out), you should look carefully for errors among the statements commented out.

These features must be used with discretion or the results are likely to be confusing, but at times they can be of great help in tracking down elusive bugs, especially in larger, complex programs.

A final word to the wise—if your program doesn't work, don't blame the computer. It is seldom at fault.

DOCUMENTATION

Programs are normally used more than once, frequently by more than one person. Program documentation consists of the various kinds of information that serve to make the purpose and use of a program clear to someone (including the programmer) who may need to use and understand it. The ideas discussed previously about program structure, comments, choice of identifier names, formatting, and the like are part of documentation. Other information normally given includes the name(s) of the programmer(s), the language and release of the language used, the date on which the program ran, the make and model of the computer used, the operating system used on the computer, a narrative discussion of what the program does and how it does it, the format required for the data (a set of sample data records with data format indicated is often helpful), a discussion of possible errors and limitations of what can be handled, descriptions of any subroutines used, a program listing with sample output, and any necessary flowcharts.

Flowcharts should take a multilevel approach for complex programs. As a general rule, a flowchart should not be larger than one standard 8½" by 11" sheet of paper. (A similar rule of thumb says that no program module should exceed one page, or about fifty statements.) If more detail is needed, it can be shown on following detail charts that expand on process boxes on higher-level charts.

Part of the documentation package should consist of instructions for nonprogrammers who will use the program. A handbook or manual describing the user interface can facilitate interaction between the operator and the program. The ideal user manual is brief, clearly written, organized, and indexed, defines unfamiliar terms, and provides examples of all procedures. While this ideal is seldom, if ever, achieved, the description suggests aspects to keep in mind when writing user documentation.

One approach to user documentation is to incorporate examples and instructions into the program, providing messages to assist users as they interact with the program. If the program runs only online, this approach is frequently implemented in a "menu-driven" interaction. The user is presented with a list of choices, and makes a selection from the list. This is in contrast to the "command-driven" interaction, in which the user must key in a syntactically correct, properly spelled and punctuated command. The menu-driven approach is sometimes referred to as "user friendly"; it requires less previous knowledge of the program or system, but its execution may be more cumbersome than the command-driven approach.

12. Sorting

Filling the BOOKS array in SDI resulted in a sorting of book records into their respective classes. Sorting is a frequently needed operation and one for which there are many algorithms. Normally we want to sort items into ascending or descending order with each item in its ranked position rather than simply sorting items into classes.

Numbers or character strings can be sorted, and the sorting value for characters depends on the particular coding scheme used in your computer for representing the characters in binary code. The sorting process can be simple or complex, inefficient or efficient, costly or inexpensive—all depending on the output format desired, the amount of data to be processed, and the coding of the program.

The kind of sorting discussed here, one of the easiest and fastest to code, is called an exchange sort. It is adequate for small to moderate file sizes, but for big jobs it should be replaced by more efficient coding. Moroever, the simple sorting done here relies on the collating sequence of the machine; i.e., it supplies "letter by letter" output. Since the blank precedes letters and numbers in ASCII, this usually provides the "word by word" output that is often considered more elegant and useful by librarians.

A simple exchange sort can be implemented by causing the computer to compare successive pairs of elements in an array. If the items are already in the desired order, then they are left alone; if not, they are exchanged. After one pass through the array, the largest or smallest item, depending on the direction of the sort, will have "bubbled" its way to the appropriate end. When this process is repeated, the next larger or smaller item wends its way to the next extreme position, and so on until the array is ordered. Because of the way this program proceeds to its conclusion, it is often called a bubble sort.

Letters and special characters have numerical representations internal to the machine, and they can be treated as numbers in that they, too, can be used with the relational or comparison operators =, >, <, where A<B<C, etc. The final sequence of all characters and the strings formed from them are determined by the computer's collating sequence. The simple sort diagram shows how a one-dimensional array of character strings can be sorted into order using the method described (see Figure 4). Triangles are used to denote comparisons where exchanges actually take place. Circles indicate comparisons where no exchange is necessary.

PRACTICE PROBLEM NINE: SIMPLE SORTING

Write a program that will read in a random list of words and, using the exchange method, sort them into alphabetical order and then print the ordered list. It would be instructive to work through a short list manually using the algorithm before trying to write the program. The list will very likely have to be scanned more than once.

SIMPLE SORT: PROGRAM AND ANALYSIS

The crucial element in SORT is the comparison between two words. If "words[i]" is greater than (i.e., alphabetically comes after) "words[i+1]," then the two change positions. This is done by temporarily storing the contents of "words[i]" in "temp," putting "words[i+1]" in the "words[i]" position, then putting "temp" in the "words[i+1]" position.

If we were to begin with a list that was already in alphabetical order, there would be no need to go through the list more than once. We can use a flag, the Boolean variable "sorted" to note if an exchange was made on each pass through the list. When we pass through the list and "sorted" remains true, we can end the sort process.

The data file for this program is a list of names, in a file NAMES.TXT. Each name is on a separate line.

```
The Other One
Snow White
Sneezy
Sleepy
Grumpy
Dopey
Doc
Bashful
```

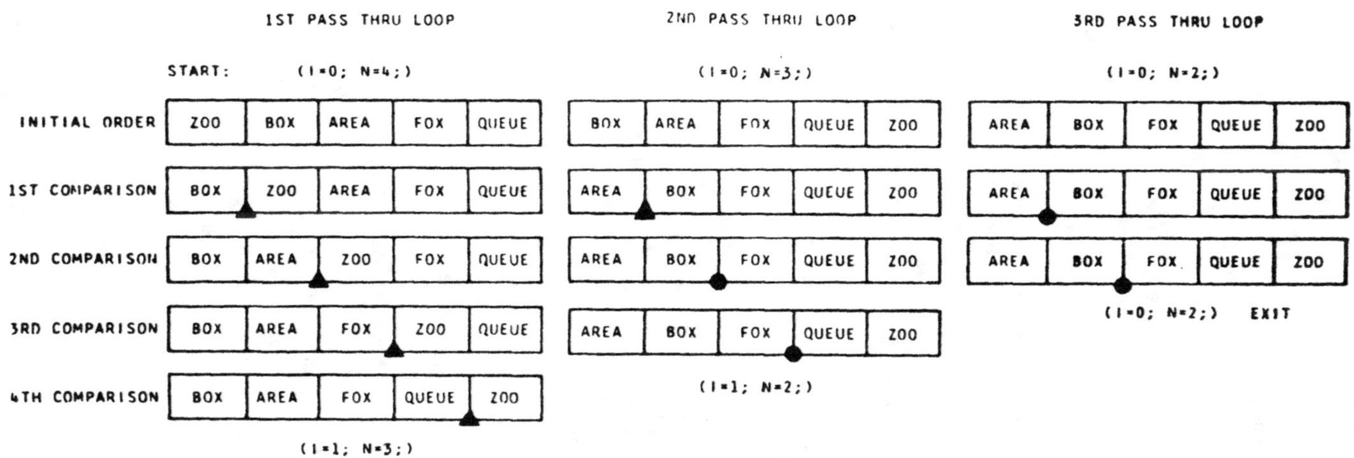

Figure 4
Sorting Diagram

The program, SORT.PAS is:

```
PROGRAM sort;
{Basic bubble, or exchange sort}
{$U+}
VAR fil : TEXT;
   filname: STRING[12];
   words: ARRAY[1..10] OF STRING[20];
   temp: STRING[20];
   i, numtosort, total: INTEGER;
   sorted: BOOLEAN;
BEGIN
   WRITELN ('Enter name of file to be sorted, e.g. names.txt');
   READLN (filname); ASSIGN (fil, filname); RESET (fil);
   total := 0;
   WHILE NOT EOF (fil) DO BEGIN
      total := total+1;
      READLN (fil, words[total]);
      END;
   numtosort := total;
   sorted := FALSE;
   WHILE NOT sorted DO BEGIN
      numtosort := numtosort - 1;
      sorted := true;
      FOR i := 1 to numtosort DO
      IF words[i] > words[i+1] THEN BEGIN
         temp := words[i];
         words[i] := words[i+1];
         words[i+1] := temp;
         sorted := FALSE;
      END;
   END;
   FOR i := 1 TO total DO
      WRITELN (words[i]);
END.
```

Output from the program is the sorted list of names:

```
Enter name of file to be sorted, e.g. names.txt
names.txt
Bashful
Doc
Dopey
Grumpy
Sleepy
Sneezy
Snow White
The Other One

>
```

The sort program is an example of a sequence of commands which can be useful as part of a larger program. The statements from the {sorting process} can be used as a sort procedure in other programs. It is wise to use formal parameters to pass the array to be sorted ("words" in this case) and the number of items ("wordcount"); otherwise it is necessary to make sure the array and variable names are the same as the names used in other parts of the program. The other variables ("i," "numtosort," "sorted," and "temp") occur only in the sort procedure. They can be declared in the procedure, but "temp" must be declared to match the elements of the array.

13. Sets and Set Operations

We have used arrays to work with a group of similar data elements. Each element of an array can be handled individually by referring to its position in the array. The Pascal "set" data type is used for a collection of similar data elements that are handled as a set. For example, we might have a set of punctuation marks, to be ignored in indexing, or a set of branch library codes. In TURBO Pascal a set may have up to 256 members, and all must be of the same type. The type for all members of a set is called the base type, and it may be byte, integer, Boolean, character, or a programmer-defined type.

SET CREATION

A set data type definition uses the reserved words TYPE and SET OF:

```
TYPE type_name = SET OF base_type;
```

We can then declare one or more variables of type type_name, whose members will be of the base type:

```
VAR set_name : type_name;
```

We assign values to each set using the assignment operator and a list of values in square brackets:

```
set_name := [value_1, value_2, . . value_n];
```

For example, if we wish to create a set of the capital letters in the first half of the alphabet and a set of capital vowels:

```
TYPE letterset = SET OF 'A' . . 'Z';
VAR firstcaps, vowels, letters: letterset;
BEGIN
  firstcaps := ['A' . . 'M'];
  vowels := ['A', 'E', 'I', 'O', 'U'];
```

SET OPERATIONS

In working with two sets we can create new sets using the union, difference, and intersection operators. Union (specified with the "+" character) creates a set of elements that are present in either or both of the original sets.

```
letters := firstcaps + vowels;
```

results in the set letters containing 'A,' 'B,' 'C,' 'D,' 'E,' 'F,' 'G,' 'H,', 'I,' 'J,' 'K,' 'L,' 'M,' 'O,' and 'U.'

Difference (−) results in a set of the elements from one set that are not present in the second.

```
letters := vowels - firstcaps;
```

assigns to the set letters 'O,' and 'U.'

Intersection (*) creates a set of elements present in both original sets.

```
letters := firstcaps * vowels;
```

sets letters equal to 'A,' 'E,' and 'I.'

Pascal uses relational operators for equality, inequality, and inclusion to compare sets; the result of such a comparison is either true or false. Set equality is specified with the = character.

```
set_1 = set_2
```

is true if every element of set_1 is a member of set_2 and every element of set_2 is a member of set_1.

Set inequality uses the <> symbol.

```
set_1 <> set _2
```

is true when there is at least one element of set_1 not in set _2, or at least one member of set_2 not in set _1.

Set inclusion indicates subsets, using the < = symbol.

set_1 < = set_2

is true if every element in set _1 is a member of set_2.

An important set operator, IN, tests for set membership. An expression of the same type as the set is evaluated and checked to see if the result is an element of the set. For example, if the variable next_char has the value 'k,'

UpCase (next_char) IN firstcaps

will be true.

TEXT PROCESSING, KEYWORD INDEXING

The next practice problems, keyword index, and keyword index using flags, illustrate the use of computers for text processing. This approach to keyword indexing takes advantage of the fact that a word in text is separated from another by a blank and possibly some punctuation.

Word indexing relies on the document as the source of index terms. Generally keyword indexes are derived from titles and sometimes other parts of the document as well, such as abstracts and/or captions for illustrations. Term selection is usually a negative process. Words judged to be generally noninformative are specified, and all others are then used as index terms. The list of non-index terms is often called a stop list. It may consist of as few as ten or twelve articles and conjunctions, or it may be a list of several hundred terms. When an entire document text is processed in this way the result is a concordance.

Keyword indexes come in two basic formats: KWIC and KWOC. These stand for "Key Word In Context" and "Key Word Out of Context." They differ in the printing format. KWOC indexes look more like conventional indexes, and are perhaps easier to read; KWIC indexes tend to keep like topics together (insofar as like topics are indicated by word pairs). The keyword indexing using flags program illustrates augmentation of the title entries, as additional terms are added to some titles to make them more informative.

These kinds of indexes typically have no vocabulary control over synonyms, homographs, and word forms; no cross-reference structure for related, broader, or narrower terms; and depend on authors for informative titles. Keyword indexes do offer a number of advantages: they are fairly inexpensive, are relatively quick and easy to produce, have no lag between when authors use new vocabulary and its inclusion in the index, provide multiple access points, and require little intellectual effort in index production.

Other forms of processing textual materials are useful. A related kind of text processing that involves word frequencies has been used by scholars to resolve questions of authorship of anonymous works and in the investigation of bibliometric phenomena, among other things.

PRACTICE PROBLEM TEN: CONVENTIONAL KEYWORD INDEXING

Write a program to produce a KWOC index. This involves reading in a stop list, then reading in a series of titles. For each title isolate each word, remove punctuation, and compare the word with the stop list. If the word is not in the stop list, use the word as an index term. Concatenate the key word with the title and store these index entries in an array. After all titles have been processed, sort the array and store the index in an output file. To make the KWOC problem more challenging, include a step to have each index term listed only once, that is, suppress printing of the key word as an index entry after its first occurrence.

The program KWOC uses procedures extensively, and some procedures have local variables—which are declared only in the procedure in which they are used. We also use the set operator IN to check to see if the last character of a potential keyword is a punctuation mark.

The data files for program KWOC are a stop list and a list of titles. The stop list, "stoplist.txt" contains:

```
TO
THE
AND
OF
IN
FOR
BY
A
AN
OR
```

The file "kwocin.txt" is a list of twelve titles:

```
SOURCES OF BUSINESS INFORMATION
THE READING OF BOOKS
GUIDE TO REFERENCE MATERIALS
INTRODUCTION TO THE LITERATURE OF EUROPE
CONSERVATION OF LIBRARY MATERIALS
THE CONSERVATION OF CULTURAL PROPERTY
ENGLISH BOOKS AND READERS
SUPPRESSED BOOKS
GUIDE TO REFERENCE BOOKS
GUIDE TO INFORMATION SCIENCE
LIBRARY AUTOMATION: THE STATE OF THE ART
THE PRIVATE LIBRARY
```

The program KWOC works with these two files:

```
PROGRAM KWOC;
{Key word index using stopword list}
{$U+}
VAR fil : TEXT;
   filname: STRING[12];
   stoplist: ARRAY[1..20] OF STRING[5];
   titlelist: ARRAY[1..100] OF STRING[100];
   word: STRING[20];
   title, temp: STRING[100];
   stopnum, ptr, entries: INTEGER;
   stopword_found: BOOLEAN;

PROCEDURE read_stoplist; {read stopwords, store count in stopnum}
BEGIN
   ASSIGN (fil, 'stoplist.txt'); RESET (fil);
   stopnum := 1;
   WHILE NOT EOF (fil) DO BEGIN
      READLN (fil, stoplist[stopnum]);
      stopnum := stopnum +1;
   END;
   WRITELN ('stoplist entered');
END; {procedure read_stoplist}

PROCEDURE find_word; {find word, remove punctuation, redefine temp}
VAR lastchar: CHAR;
BEGIN
   {remove leading blanks}
   WHILE POS (' ', temp) = 1 DO
      temp := COPY (temp, 2, LENGTH (temp)-1);
   {copy everything up to blank into word}
   ptr := POS (' ', temp);
   IF ptr > 0 THEN BEGIN
      word := COPY (temp, 1, ptr-1);
      temp := COPY (temp, ptr+1, (LENGTH (temp)-LENGTH(word)+1));
      END
   ELSE word := temp; {last word in title}
   {remove punctuation at end of word}
   lastchar := COPY (word, LENGTH (word), 1);
   IF lastchar IN ['!', ',', ':', ';', '.']  THEN
      word := COPY (word, 1, LENGTH (word)-1);
   END; {procedure find_word}
```

```
PROCEDURE check_stop; {compare word with stoplist}
VAR i: INTEGER;
BEGIN
stopword_found := FALSE;
FOR i := 1 to stopnum DO
   IF word = stoplist [i] THEN stopword_found := TRUE;
END; {procedure stop_check}

PROCEDURE save_entry; {add keyword and title to titlelist}
VAR i, numblanks: INTEGER;
BEGIN
    entries := entries +1;
    {pad word with blanks before concatenating with title}
    numblanks := 20 - LENGTH (word);
    FOR i := 1 TO numblanks DO word := CONCAT (word, ' ');
    titlelist[entries] := CONCAT (word, title);
END; {procedure save_entry}

PROCEDURE sort_it; {exchange sort for titlelist}
CONST twentyblanks='
VAR i, numtosort: INTEGER;
   sorted: BOOLEAN;
BEGIN
   numtosort := entries;
   sorted := FALSE;
   WHILE NOT sorted DO BEGIN
      numtosort := numtosort - 1;
      sorted := true;
      FOR i := 1 to numtosort DO
      IF titlelist [i] > titlelist [i+1] THEN BEGIN
         temp := titlelist[i];
         titlelist[i] := titlelist [i+1];
         titlelist [i+1] := temp;
         sorted := FALSE;
      END;
   END; {titlelist sorted}
   {suppress printing of duplicate key words in index}
   FOR i := entries-1 DOWNTO 2 DO
      IF COPY (titlelist[i], 1, 20) = COPY (titlelist [i-1], 1, 20) THEN
         titlelist [i] := CONCAT (twentyblanks,
                           COPY (titlelist[i], 21, LENGTH (titlelist[i])));
END; {procedure sort_it}

PROCEDURE write_out;
VAR outfil: TEXT;
   i: INTEGER;
BEGIN
   ASSIGN (outfil, 'KWOCOUT.TXT'); REWRITE (outfil);
   FOR i := 1 TO entries DO
      WRITELN (outfil, titlelist[i]);
   CLOSE (outfil);
  WRITELN ('KWOC index written to file KWOCOUT.TXT');
END; {procedure write_out}

{main program}
BEGIN
   read_stoplist;
   WRITELN ('Enter name of key word index data file, e.g., KWOCIN.TXT');
   READLN (filname); ASSIGN (fil, filname); RESET (fil);
   entries := 0;
```

```
   WHILE NOT EOF (fil) DO BEGIN
      READLN (fil, title);
      temp := title;
      ptr := 1;
      WHILE ptr > 0 DO BEGIN
         find_word;
         check_stop;
         IF NOT stopword_found THEN save_entry;
      END;
   END; {end of input file processing}
   sort_it;
   write_out;
END.
```

Note the final statement of procedure sort_it, to suppress printing of duplicate index terms. The secret is to scan the sorted array from the bottom up, replacing any but the first occurrence of the index term with blanks. Sorting from the bottom up is done using DOWNTO in the final loop of procedure sort_it. The statement begins:

FOR i := entries DOWNTO 2 DO

The initial value of "i" is set to the position of the last entry, and "i" is decremented (one is subtracted from "i") on each pass through the loop until "i" reaches the final value of two.

Output from program KWOC, written to the file kwocout.txt, is:

```
ART             LIBRARY AUTOMATION: THE STATE OF THE ART
AUTOMATION      LIBRARY AUTOMATION: THE STATE OF THE ART
BOOKS           ENGLISH BOOKS AND READERS
                GUIDE TO REFERENCE BOOKS
                SUPPRESSED BOOKS
                THE READING OF BOOKS
BUSINESS        SOURCES OF BUSINESS INFORMATION
CONSERVATION    CONSERVATION OF LIBRARY MATERIALS
                THE CONSERVATION OF CULTURAL PROPERTY
CULTURAL        THE CONSERVATION OF CULTURAL PROPERTY
ENGLISH         ENGLISH BOOKS AND READERS
EUROPE          INTRODUCTION TO THE LITERATURE OF EUROPE
GUIDE           GUIDE TO INFORMATION SCIENCE
                GUIDE TO REFERENCE BOOKS
                GUIDE TO REFERENCE MATERIALS
INFORMATION     GUIDE TO INFORMATION SCIENCE
                SOURCES OF BUSINESS INFORMATION
INTRODUCTION    INTRODUCTION TO THE LITERATURE OF EUROPE
LIBRARY         CONSERVATION OF LIBRARY MATERIALS
                LIBRARY AUTOMATION: THE STATE OF THE ART
                THE PRIVATE LIBRARY
LITERATURE      INTRODUCTION TO THE LITERATURE OF EUROPE
MATERIALS       CONSERVATION OF LIBRARY MATERIALS
                GUIDE TO REFERENCE MATERIALS
```

```
PRIVATE            THE PRIVATE LIBRARY
PROPERTY           THE CONSERVATION OF CULTURAL PROPERTY
READERS            ENGLISH BOOKS AND READERS
READING            THE READING OF BOOKS
REFERENCE          GUIDE TO REFERENCE BOOKS
                   GUIDE TO REFERENCE MATERIALS
SCIENCE            GUIDE TO INFORMATION SCIENCE
SOURCES            SOURCES OF BUSINESS INFORMATION
STATE              LIBRARY AUTOMATION: THE STATE OF THE ART
SUPPRESSED         SUPPRESSED BOOKS
```

PRACTICE PROBLEM ELEVEN: KEYWORD INDEXING USING FLAGS

Conventional keyword indexes work best in subject areas in which long, accurate, and informative titles can reasonably be expected, as in the sciences. In many types of publications we cannot be sure of obtaining this type of title. Newspaper articles, for instance, generally have short, catchy titles that would not produce useful keyword indexes.

For such documents we can vary the KWOC program to do keyword indexing using flags. Here special characters, or flags, are used to mark words or phrases to be used as index entries. In addition to title words, other informative words and phrases may be added to augment the information contained in the title. These added terms must also be flagged. This approach combines human judgment with the manipulative capabilities of the computer to produce the index.

For this problem you are to write a program that will identify character strings between two flags (special characters such as * and /, for instance). Use the terms identified in this way to construct the KWOC index. Concatenate each index term with its cleaned-up title (without flags), then sort and store the results in an output file.

The input for this program, 'flagsin.txt,' is:

```
85-22723   *DEBUGGING/: A *GUIDE/ TO *HAWAIIAN LIVING/
85-22813   THIS DOES NOT *COMPUTE/
85-23667   WHO PUT THE *INPUT/ IN THE *OUTPUT/?
85-51397   HOW TO COPE WITH *FATAL ERRORS/
85-81462   USING *TURBO PASCAL/ IN THE *REAL WORLD/
85-84238   *FATAL ERRORS/ IN THE *DEBUGGING/ PROCESS
85-88206   TO *COMPUTE/ OR NOT TO COMPUTE
85-88300   BLAISING SADDLES *PASCAL, BLAISE/ *FICTION/
```

The program FLAGS is a variation of KWOC. FLAGS is a shorter progam, since the identification of index terms is accomplished before the data file is prepared.

```
PROGRAM flags;
{Key word index using flags to indicate words to be indexed}
{$U+}
VAR fil : TEXT;
   filname: STRING[12];
   titlelist: ARRAY[1..100] OF STRING[100];
   keywords: ARRAY[1..10] OF STRING[40];
   word: STRING[40];
   title : STRING[100];
   keys, entries: INTEGER;

PROCEDURE find_word;
{find flagged term in title, redefine title to remove flag}
VAR star, slash, last: INTEGER;
   firstpart, lastpart: STRING[100];
BEGIN
   star := POS ('*', title);
   slash := POS ('/', title);
   last := slash - (star + 1);
   IF star > 1 THEN firstpart := COPY (title, 1, star-1)
      ELSE firstpart := '';
   word := COPY (title, star + 1, last);
   lastpart := COPY (title, slash + 1, LENGTH (title) - slash + 1);
   title := CONCAT (firstpart, word, lastpart);
   {save keyword}
   keys := keys +1;
   keywords[keys] := word;
END; {procedure find_word}

PROCEDURE save_entry; {add keyword and title to titlelist}
VAR i, j, numblanks: INTEGER;
BEGIN
   FOR i := 1 TO keys DO BEGIN
      entries := entries + 1;
      {pad keyword with blanks before concatenation with title}
      numblanks := 20 - LENGTH (keywords[i]);
      FOR j := 1 TO numblanks DO
         keywords[i] := CONCAT (keywords[i], ' ');
      titlelist[entries] := CONCAT (keywords[i], title);
   END;
END; {procedure save_entry}

PROCEDURE sort_it; {exchange sort for titlelist}
CONST twentyblanks='                    ';
VAR i, numtosort: INTEGER;
   sorted: BOOLEAN;
BEGIN
   numtosort := entries;
   sorted := FALSE;
   WHILE NOT sorted DO BEGIN
      numtosort := numtosort - 1;
      sorted := true;
      FOR i := 1 to numtosort DO
      IF titlelist [i] > titlelist [i+1] THEN BEGIN
         title := titlelist[i];

      titlelist[i] := titlelist [i+1];
      titlelist [i+1] := title;
      sorted := FALSE;
   END;
```

```
   END; {titlelist sorted}
   {suppress printing of duplicate key words in index}
   FOR i := entries DOWNTO 2 DO
      IF COPY (titlelist[i], 1, 20) = COPY (titlelist [i-1], 1, 20)
         THEN titlelist [i] := CONCAT (twentyblanks,
         COPY (titlelist[i], 21, LENGTH (titlelist[i])));
END; {procedure sort_it}

PROCEDURE write_out;
VAR outfil: TEXT;
   i: INTEGER;
BEGIN
   ASSIGN (outfil, 'FLAGSOUT.TXT'); REWRITE (outfil);
   FOR i := 1 TO entries DO
      WRITELN (outfil, titlelist[i]);
   CLOSE (outfil);
  WRITELN ('KWOC index written to file FLAGSOUT.TXT');
END; {procedure write_out}

{main program}
BEGIN
   WRITELN ('Enter key word index file, e.g., FLAGSIN.TXT');
   READLN (filname); ASSIGN (fil, filname); RESET (fil);
   entries := 0;
   WHILE NOT EOF (fil) DO BEGIN
      READLN (fil, title);
      keys := 0;
      WHILE POS ('*', title) > 0 DO find_word;
      save_entry;
   END;
   sort_it;
   write_out;
END.
```

The output file, "flagsout.txt," contains the index:

```
COMPUTE             85-22813   THIS DOES NOT COMPUTE
                    85-88206   TO COMPUTE OR NOT TO COMPUTE
DEBUGGING           85-22723   DEBUGGING: A GUIDE TO HAWAIIAN LIVING
                    85-84238   FATAL ERRORS IN THE DEBUGGING PROCESS
FATAL ERRORS        85-51397   HOW TO COPE WITH FATAL ERRORS
                    85-84238   FATAL ERRORS IN THE DEBUGGING PROCESS
FICTION             85-88300   BLAISING SADDLES PASCAL, BLAISE FICTION
GUIDE               85-22723   DEBUGGING: A GUIDE TO HAWAIIAN LIVING
HAWAIIAN LIVING     85-22723   DEBUGGING: A GUIDE TO HAWAIIAN LIVING
INPUT               85-23667   WHO PUT THE INPUT IN THE OUTPUT?
OUTPUT              85-23667   WHO PUT THE INPUT IN THE OUTPUT?
PASCAL, BLAISE      85-88300   BLAISING SADDLES PASCAL, BLAISE FICTION
REAL WORLD          85-81462   USING TURBO PASCAL IN THE REAL WORLD
TURBO PASCAL        85-81462   USING TURBO PASCAL IN THE REAL WORLD
```

14. Records; Interactive Programs

RECORDS

Arrays are useful data structures for a group of elements all of the same type. For a collection of data elements of varying types, TURBO Pascal uses a structure called a "record." A record consists of a fixed number of fields, which may be of different types. The record type definition gives the name of the record type, the reserved word RECORD, and a list of the field names and field types. The record type definition is concluded with the word END:

```
TYPE type_name = RECORD
  field_name_1 : type_1;
  field_name_2 : type_2;
  ...
END;
```

The following example gives the definition for a record to handle bibliographic information for books:

```
TYPE bookrecord = RECORD
  author : STRING[30];
  title : STRING[120];
  publ : STRING[40];
  year : integer;
END;
```

It is possible to create an array of records, as a subsequent part of the type definition:

```
bookarray: ARRAY[1..25] OF bookrecord;
```

Once the types are defined we can declare variables to represent the record and an array of bookrecords:

```
VAR onebook : bookrecord;
  books : bookarray;
```

To refer to fields within a record give the record name, a period (full stop), then the field name. To assign a title to the title field of the variable onebook:

```
onebook.title := 'My first book of programming';
```

Working with an array of records requires one to use the array name, the subscript for the desired record in the array, a period, then the name of the field:

```
books[count].publ := 'Greenwood';
```

INTERACTIVE PROGRAMS

In previous programs we relied on the user to enter the name of the text or data files to be processed. At times it is desirable to have users enter data from the keyboard rather than by storing it in a separate file. Programs allowing this kind of interaction need to do at least two things: prompt the user to enter the information and be sufficiently "robust" to handle a variety of entries from users.

As we have seen, user prompts can be given through WRITELN commands to display information on the screen. Prompts should give brief, clear instructions and may include examples and/or give directions on how to request help or exit the program.

Program "robustness" to accommodate a variety of user actions can never be perfect, but common problems can be anticipated and their effects prevented. For example, a program can read what the user types and check it against acceptable responses. If the response is not acceptable the program can give the prompt again or provide more detailed instructions.

PRACTICE PROBLEM TWELVE: BIBLIOGRAPHY

Write an interactive program to read book records entered from the keyboard, sort them by author, write the sorted bibliography to an output file, and print the file.

```
program Bibliog(input, output, ExternalFile);
{Accepts book records, sorts them by author, writes the sorted}
{bibliography to a text file, then lists the file to verify that}
{it worked.     Written by G. Lundeen 12/4/84}
{$U+}

Const MaxBooks = 10;     {how many records in file}

Type BookRecord = Record
                   Author: string[30];
                   Title : string[120];
                   Publ  : string[40];
                   Year  : integer;
                  end;
     BookArray = Array[1..MaxBooks] of BookRecord;
     TagArray = Array[1..MaxBooks] of integer;
     KeyString = string[30];
     FilVar = text;

Var I,
    Count: integer;          {How many books so far}
    Tag: TagArray;           {array of tags pointing to BookArray}
    Book: BookArray;         {BookRecords in order of entry}
    ExternalFile: FilVar;    {Name of external text file}
    Line: string[120];       {string variable for writing out file}
                             {to screen}

{*****************************************************************}
{Modified insertion sort, inserts tag pointing to main array}
{contains function Upper to convert strings to upper case}
procedure sort(VAR Key  : KeyString;
               VAR Book : BookArray;
               VAR Tag  : TagArray;
               VAR Count: integer);


VAR I: integer;
{*****************************************************}
Function Upper(st:KeyString):KeyString;
 Var I: integer;
 Begin
   for I := 1 to length(st) do
    st[I] := UpCase(st[I]);

   Upper := st;
 end;
{*****************************************************}
begin {sort}
     I := Count - 1;
     while (Upper(Book[Tag[I]].Author) > Upper(Key)) and (I > 0) do
        begin
           Tag[I + 1] := Tag[I];
           I := I - 1;
        end;
        Tag[I + 1] := Count;
 end; {sort}
```

```
{**********************************************************}
{Prompts for input of fields in record}
procedure GetBook( VAR Book: BookRecord);
Begin
     writeln('Author: ');
     readln(Book.Author);
     if Book.Author <> ''   {quit if no author entered}
       then
         begin
           writeln('Title: ');
           readln(Book.Title);
           writeln('Publisher: ');
           readln(Book.Publ);
           writeln('Year: ');
           readln(Book.Year);
         end;
end;
{**********************************************************}
{writes record to external file}
Procedure PutBook(VAR Book: BookRecord; VAR FileName: FilVar);
Begin
   With Book do
     Begin
        Writeln(FileName, Author);
        Writeln(FileName, Title);
        Writeln(FileName, Publ);
        Writeln(FileName, Year);
     end;
end;
{**********************************************************}
                   { MAIN MODULE }
Begin {bibliog}

   Writeln('Enter records one field at a time, up to ',MaxBooks);
   Writeln('If you have fewer than ', MaxBooks, ' records end`);
   Writeln('with an empty return when asked for the next author.');
   Writeln;
   GetBook(Book[1]);
   Count := 1;
   While (Book[Count].Author <> '') and (Count <= MaxBooks) do
     Begin
        Sort(Book[Count].Author,Book,Tag,Count);
        Count := Count + 1;
        If Count <= MaxBooks
           then  GetBook(Book[Count]);
     end;
     Count := Count - 1;    {Correct for counting one too many}

{write records to external text file}
    assign(ExternalFile,'BOOKS.DAT');
    Rewrite(ExternalFile);
    for I := 1 to Count do
        PutBook(Book[Tag[I]],ExternalFile);
    close(ExternalFile);
```

```
{List the file contents on the screen}
   Reset(ExternalFile);
   While not EOF(ExternalFile) do
     Begin
        Readln(ExternalFile,Line);
        Writeln(line);
     end;
end.
```

INSERTION SORT

Program BIBLIOG uses an insertion sort routine. The main array of books is maintained in its original order, and a separate array of tags is used to indicate the order in which the books should be printed. This approach to sorting means that the records do not need to be copied and recopied—rather, the values in the tags array are changed if items are added or removed and the books array is resorted.

An example of the output from BIBLIOG.PAS is given below:

```
Enter records one field at a time, up to 10
If you have fewer than 10 records end
with an empty return when asked for the next author.

Author: Dui, Melvil
Title: How to Manage a Library Good
Publisher: Vanity Press
Year: 1877
Author: Ho, Ed
Title: Administration of Libraries
Publisher: Power Press
Year: 1990
Author: Barnard, C.
Title: Surgery for Lefthanders
Publisher: Shoelace
Year: 1970
Author:

Barnard, C.
Surgery for Lefthanders
Shoelace
1970
Dui, Melvil
How to Manage a Library Good
Vanity Press
1877
```

```
Ho, Ed
Administration of Libraries
Power Press
1990
```

A SAMPLE STUDENT PROGRAM: DOCUMENT RETRIEVAL USING WEIGHTED-TERM LOGIC

Weighted-term search logic is really an offshoot of the familiar AND, OR, and NOT logic derived from Boolean algebra. As such, it provides a means for coordinating terms under which documents have been indexed, or, if the documents have not been indexed, it allows coordination of terms from titles or text—a technique called free text searching.

In its simplest form, weighted-term logic permits the searcher to assign small integer numbers to the desired terms. If an individual term is found, its weight is compared with a threshold value that was chosen by the searcher. If the term weight is greater than or equal to the threshold value, then the data associated with the document are displayed, printed, or otherwise handled through an output channel. Otherwise, the data are ignored and the next record is searched. If more than one term is found, all term weights are summed by the computer and there is a comparison between the combined weight and the threshold value. By assigning each term a weight greater than or equal to the threshold value, one ensures a logical OR relationship. If only the sums of the terms' weights provide a "hit," then logical AND will have been simulated. Logical NOT can be achieved by setting one term's weight equal to the threshold value, while the weights of undesired terms are set at minus one or at any other negative number within the limits of the system. Exclusive OR can be simulated by using a negative threshold value and negative weights for individual terms that are set equal to the threshold.

The principal advantage of weighted-term searching is that the searcher can assign weights that are directly proportional to values placed on individual terms—the more valuable, the higher the weights. In addition, the sum of these weights gives a total value for each document that is probably an indication of its relevance. By printing these sums in addition to data about the document, one can help identify the most interesting documents quickly. It is also possible, of course, to produce a sort based on these document weights, so that one can display the records in decreasing order of probable relevance.

Sample file BIOMAGS. TXT:

```
ACUTE CARE
ADVANCES IN ENZYME REGULATION
AMERICAN BIRDS
AMERICAN JOURNAL OF ANATOMY
```

AMERICAN ENTOMOLOGICAL SOCIETY TRANSACTIONS
AMERICAN JOURNAL OF BOTANY
AMERICAN JOURNAL OF EPIDEMIOLOGY
AMERICAN JOURNAL OF NURSING
AMERICAN JOURNAL OF PHYSIOLOGY
AMERICAN NATURALIST
AMERICAN PHARMACY
AMERICAN SCIENTIST
AMERICAN ZOOLOGIST
ANALYTICAL BIOCHEMISTRY
ANATOMICAL RECORD
ANIMAL BEHAVIOR ABSTRACTS
ANIMAL KINGDOM
ANNALS OF BOTANY
ANTARCTIC BIBLIOGRAPHY
APPLIED AND ENVIRONMENTAL MICROBIOLOGY
AQUATIC BOTANY
ARCHIVES OF BIOCHEMISTRY AND BIOPHYSICS

The TURBO Pascal program:

```
PROGRAM weight ;  {Weighted-term search program}
  {Gerald M. Carlson
   August 6, 1987}

TYPE TitleType = STRING [80] ;
     TermType = STRING [40] ;

VAR filname : STRING [12] ;
fil : TEXT ;
TitleNum, Thresh, TermNum, i, j : INTEGER ;
Search : CHAR ;
Title : ARRAY [1..40] OF TitleType ;
Term : ARRAY [1..10] OF TermType ;
Weight : ARRAY [1..10] OF INTEGER ;
DocWt : ARRAY [1..40] OF INTEGER ;
Found : BOOLEAN ;

FUNCTION upper (instring : TermType) : TermType ;
  VAR k : INTEGER ;
BEGIN {upper}
    FOR k := 1 TO LENGTH (instring) DO
      instring [k] := UPCASE (instring [k]) ;
    upper := instring ;
END ;  {upper}

BEGIN  {Main program}
 WRITELN ('Enter name of file to be searched, e.g., BIOMAGS.TXT') ;
 READLN (filname) ; ASSIGN (fil, filname) ; RESET (fil) ;

  {Read in list of titles and count them}
TitleNum := 0 ;
WHILE NOT EOF (fil) DO BEGIN
  TitleNum := TitleNum + 1 ;
  READLN (fil, Title [TitleNum]) ;
END ;  {WHILE}
```

```
Search := 'Y';
WHILE (Search = 'Y') OR (Search = 'y') DO BEGIN

   {Get weight threshold, terms and weights from user}
 WRITE ('Enter number of terms to be searched:') ;
 READLN (TermNum) ;
 WRITE ('Enter document weight threshold: ') ;
 READLN (Thresh) ;
 WRITELN ('Enter search terms and weights:') ;
 FOR i := 1 TO TermNum DO BEGIN
   WRITE ('Term ', i, ': ') ; READ (Term [i]) ;
   WRITE ('      Weight: ') ; READLN (Weight [i]) ;
 END ;  {FOR i}

 IF TermNum = 10 THEN WRITE ('Capacity of ten terms reached.  ') ;

   {Search title list for terms, compare weights to threshold, and
     write out hits}
 WRITELN ('Commencing search of ', filname) ; WRITELN ;
 Found := FALSE ;
 FOR i := 1 TO TitleNum DO BEGIN
   DocWt [i] := 0 ;
   FOR j := 1 to TermNum DO
     IF POS (Upper (Term [j]), Title [i]) <> 0
           THEN DocWt [i] := DocWt [i] + Weight [j] ;
   IF (DocWt [i] >= Thresh) AND (DocWt [i] <> 0) THEN BEGIN
     WRITELN (Title [i]) ;
     Found := TRUE ;
   END ;  {IF}
 END ; {FOR i}
 WRITELN ('Search completed.') ;
 IF NOT Found THEN WRITELN ('No items found.') ;
 WRITELN ;
 WRITE ('Another search? (Enter Y/N)') ; READLN (Search) ;
END ;  {WHILE Search}
WRITELN ('Good-Bye!') ;
END.  {WEIGHT}
```

An interaction at the computer:

```
Enter name of file to be searched, e.g., BIOMAGS.TXT
Biomags.txt
Enter number of terms to be searched:2
Enter document weight threshold: 5
Enter search terms and weights:
Term 1: american     Weight: 3
Term 2: journal     Weight: 3
Commencing search of biomags.txt

AMERICAN JOURNAL OF ANATOMY
AMERICAN JOURNAL OF BOTANY
AMERICAN JOURNAL OF EPIDEMIOLOGY
AMERICAN JOURNAL OF NURSING
AMERICAN JOURNAL OF PHYSIOLOGY
AMERICAN JOURNAL OF TROPICAL MEDICINE AND HYGIENE
Search completed.
```

```
Another search? (Enter Y/N)y
Enter number of terms to be searched:2
Enter document weight threshold: 5
Enter search terms and weights:
Term 1: american     Weight: 5
Term 2: journal     Weight: -2
Commencing search of biomags.txt

AMERICAN BIRDS
AMERICAN ENTOMOLOGICAL SOCIETY TRANSACTIONS
AMERICAN NATURALIST
AMERICAN PHARMACY
AMERICAN SCIENTIST
AMERICAN ZOOLOGIST
Search completed.

Another search? (Enter Y/N)y
Enter number of terms to be searched:1
Enter document weight threshold: 5
Enter search terms and weights:
Term 1: botan     Weight: 5

AMERICAN JOURNAL OF BOTANY
ANNALS OF BOTANY
AQUATIC BOTANY
Search completed.


Another search? (Enter Y/N)y
Enter number of terms to be searched:5
Enter document weight threshold: 5
Enter search terms and weights:
Term 1: american     Weight: 1
Term 2: journal     Weight: 1
Term 3: medicine     Weight: 1
Term 4: tropical     Weight: 1
Term 5: hygiene    Weight: 1
Commencing search of biomags.txt

AMERICAN JOURNAL OF TROPICAL MEDICINE AND HYGIENE
Search completed.

Another search? (Enter Y/N)n
Good-Bye!
```

This program was adapted by Mr. Carlson from the weighted-term programs appearing in Davis and Lundeen, *Illustrative Computer Programming for Libraries: Selected Examples for Information Specialists*, 2d edition (Greenwood Press, 1981, pp. 116-119). The original programs were written in the language PL/I and required "translation" and adaptation to take advantage of the special features of Pascal.

Two final notes should be made about weighted-term searching: (1) Term truncation is highly appropriate—the second search, for example, uses the term 'botan,' which would cover all words with that stem, such as 'botany,' 'botanical,' and so forth. And (2) using small integers it is not always possible to determine from the output which terms are responsible for causing documents to be retrieved; therefore, it may be desirable to employ special procedures such as the assignment of different powers of two to terms so that unique document weights result. Procedures like this can greatly facilitate search analysis. Interested readers are referred to Chapter 5, "General Principles of Retrieval Systems," in *Guide to Information Science* by Davis and Rush (Greenwood Press, 1979, pp. 61-82), and to the work of H. P. Iker, "Solution of Boolean Equations Through Use of Term Weights to the Base Two" (*American Documentation* 18 [1967]:47).

Selected Bibliography

Davis, Charles H. and Gerald W. Lundeen. *Illustrative Computer Programming for Libraries: Selected Examples for Information Specialists*, 2nd. ed. Westport, Conn.: Greenwood Press, 1981.

Davis, Charles H. and James E. Rush. *Guide to Information Science*. Westport, Conn.: Greenwood Press, 1979.

Jensen, Kathleen and Niklaus Wirth. *Pascal User Manual and Report*, 3rd ed. New York: Springer-Verlag, 1985.

Sammet, Jean. *Programming Languages: History and Fundamentals*. Englewood Cliffs, N.J.: Prentice-Hall, 1969.

Savitch, Walter J. *An Introduction to the Art and Science of Programming: TURBO Pascal Edition*. Menlo Park, Calif.: Benjamin/Cummings Publishing Company, 1986.

Schneider, G. Michael, Steven W. Weingart, and David M. Perlman. *An Introduction to Programming and Problem Solving with Pascal*. New York: John Wiley, 1978.

Sippl, Charles J. and Charles P. Sippl. *Computer Dictionary and Handbook*, 3rd. ed. Indianapolis: Howard W. Sams, 1980.

Turbo Pascal: Reference Manual, version 3.0. Scotts Valley, Calif.: Borland International, 1985.

Turbo Tutor: A Self-Study Guide to Turbo Pascal. Scotts Valley, Calif.: Borland International, 1986.

Welsh, Jim and John Elder. *Introduction to Pascal*, 2nd. ed. Englewood Cliffs, N.J.: Prentice-Hall, 1982.

Index

About the Authors

CHARLES H. DAVIS is a Professor in the Graduate School of Library and Information Science at the University of Illinois at Urbana-Champaign. He is also Adjunct Professor at Indiana University in Bloomington.

GERALD W. LUNDEEN is a Professor in the Graduate School of Library Studies at the University of Hawaii.

DEBORA SHAW is an Assistant Professor in the School of Library and Information Science at Indiana University in Bloomington.

www.ingramcontent.com/pod-product-compliance
Lightning Source LLC
LaVergne TN
LVHW020055220926
848484LV00003BA/787
* 9 7 8 0 3 1 3 2 5 2 5 9 4 *